MARY,
Worthy of All Praise

Reflections
on the Virgin Mary
based on the Paraklesis Service

by David R. Smith

CONCILIAR PRESS

Ben Lomond, California

MARY, WORTHY OF ALL PRAISE:
Reflections on the Virgin Mary
© Copyright 2004 by David R. Smith

Published by   Conciliar Press
P.O. Box 76
Ben Lomond, California 95005-0076

Printed in the United States of America

ISBN 1-888212-71-3

Manufactured under the direction of Double Eagle Industries.
For manufacturing details, call 888-824-4344
or e-mail to info@publishingquest.com

To Dr. William Bush, my Orthodox seminary

My sincerest thanks go to Fr. Terence Baz
for his help with the manuscript,
and to my wife Donna for her
marvelous companionship and support.

Contents

Introduction

Every generation of Christians must make Mary—the Theotokos and Mother of our Lord, the bride of God, the giver of the Giver of Life, the pioneer of Christians—their own. Every culture must confront her mystery, must consider the circumstances of her pregnancy and birthgiving. Every Christian must face the debt we have to her. Every eye must gaze upon her face, as He did and does even yet, with love. Every heart must choose her, as God the Father chose her. No matter in what age we live, we must encounter the worthiness of Mary, and give her our praise.

The Church gives us many opportunities to do this, to bring ourselves to consider the place of the Mother of Jesus Christ in our lives. No one is better than any other, but I have to admit that the Paraklesis has, more than any other service in the Church, fostered in me a great love for the Theotokos. The Paraklesis is a supplicatory song, a canon of praise, a collection of eight odes of love, a series of poems celebrating with honor the Mother of Jesus our Lord. We sing the Paraklesis in the Orthodox Church every day during the Virgin's Lent, from the first to the fifteenth of August, and at other times as needed, in times of illness and distress. But many Orthodox have come to sing it much more often than that, and some pray the words of the Paraklesis every day.

I don't intend to add anything to the Church's theology of the Mother of God, because the attempt to be original has led many Christians toward error. But I want to do more than mimic the devotion to the Theotokos that previous generations had. I want to ask myself: How do I, in this time and in this place, encounter Mary? Yes, I'll use the services of the Church, unchanged and unadorned. But I want to spend time thinking about the words and images, the assertions and truth. I want to use the words and music to put Mary in my life.

These meditations do not express the sentiments of anyone except myself. But to the degree that you have the same longing to make the Theotokos a part of your life, I invite you to enjoy and benefit from them.

Although I do not associate the Paraklesis with any one time of the year, I most certainly associate the first two weeks of August with the Paraklesis. During this period, sometimes called the Virgin's Lent, many Orthodox churches sing the Paraklesis every day in preparation for the most important feast of the Theotokos, the Dormition.

Because of this, I have included here three more meditations related to the Paraklesis: the first on the spiritual discipline of fasting, the second on the Feast of the Dormition, and the third on a major feast of the Church that comes every year during the Virgin's Lent, the Transfiguration of our Lord.

Chapter One

Most Holy Theotokos, save us!

When we pray the supplications of the Paraklesis, we sing the phrase, "Most Holy Theotokos, save us!" more than any other. Let's look carefully at this phrase, what it means and what it does not mean.

Some years ago, I attended a missions and evangelism conference for Orthodox Christians. What a great blessing it was to gather together with people from my Church who long to share the good news of salvation in Jesus Christ with the whole world! I attended one session dealing with visitors to our churches where the speaker made some great suggestions—but at one point he said, "Make sure you don't sing, 'Most Holy Theotokos, save us,' at the end of Vespers when you have visitors." I was horrified at his words, but not as horrified as I was when the whole audience seemed to agree with him. Why would we change the services of the Church when we have visitors? Would we revert to singing all the words of the Vespers service when we don't have visitors? Would we also cut parts of the Divine Liturgy for the sake of visitors?

I asked the speaker later what he meant by his remark, and he told me that seekers from certain denominations might misunderstand the phrase, and might think that the Orthodox believe that Mary saves us. I tried to talk to him about the integrity of the services of the Church, but he wouldn't listen.

I can understand his point (although certainly not his conclusion!). What do these words mean, and why do they appear so often? Various services contain this phrase, just as our churches contain various icons of the Theotokos, because "Most Holy Theotokos, save us!" is in fact itself an icon in words. Just as the icons might appear a little odd to a visitor (or to anyone who thinks of them as nothing more than paintings of historical figures), so the phrase, "Most Holy Theotokos, save us!" takes some effort to understand. But certainly, the effort is well worthwhile, because this icon in words paints for us the supreme value of the Mother of God.

No Orthodox Christian would say that we sing this phrase in order to ask Mary for the eternal salvation of our souls, for "there is no other name under heaven given among men by which we must be saved" (Acts 4:12) than that of Jesus Christ our Lord. When we say, "Most Holy Theotokos, save us," we don't mean "save our souls" or "forgive us our sins." We mean something else—something that we may find ourselves uncomfortable saying: "Help me. Rescue me." We need Jesus, and she has Him. She possesses our salvation in a way that no other human being can possess Him, and so we honor her and set her in her proper place by expressing often that we need her attention, her help, her prayers, her love, her Son.

We cry out for help when we sing the phrase, "Most Holy Theotokos, save us!" in a way similar to the way we call on a dentist or doctor to find relief from pain. When we call to make an appointment, we're saying, "You have the expertise, the equipment, the medication I need to stop hurting—help me!" (At least, this is what we mean, although our words probably don't sound so desperate.) But our phone call to a doctor also differs from our cry to the Mother of God, because we regard physical pain as a force outside ourselves—and we see no humiliation in admitting that a doctor or dentist can help. Even if the doctor says we eat or drink too much, that our pain results from the way we live and bad decisions we've made, it does not approach the extremely personal nature of our cry to the Theotokos. When we plead with her to save us, we admit a deficiency in the essence of our being. We admit that we cannot, no matter what training or equipment we might employ, help ourselves. We cry to Mary from a state of utter helplessness. And when we do, we say to her, "We are totally unable to help ourselves, and only in your gift to the world can we find any hope at all. We admit no strength of our own, no value of our own, no ability to withstand the penalty of sin, no answers to our problems. We have no one to blame except ourselves, and we have no one to call out to other than you." We shout our desperation to the Theotokos, admitting not only that we need Jesus, but more—that we don't have the ability, wisdom, courage, even the insight to make Him our own.

Do you feel uncomfortable because of the extreme nature of these words? When you read them, a voice inside you may say, "Wait a minute. I'm a good person, I'm a capable person who can withstand sin by my intelligence and determination." You may think no voice inside you says this, but this probably means that the voice has become so loud that you cannot hear it. Every human feels uncomfortable with the idea that he needs to be saved. We don't want to be pitiful, pathetic, desperate, and miserable. In our day and in our society, we embrace dignity and self-esteem more than we seek God, to the degree that many of us cannot imagine that anyone would question the value of these concepts. Can we really know God, however, while we think that our own thoughts, desires, and values must automatically also be His? When we think ourselves worthy of God's love, do we not therefore remain closed to it?

There are two heretical tendencies in North American Christianity. One places Jesus Christ too far toward the human extreme, as did the ancient Arian heresy, and the other denies His humanity. "Jesus" for this second extreme becomes a concept, a philosophy, a mantra, a tool distinct from the Person of Jesus Christ our Lord. In this way of thinking, we look to "Jesus" for salvation the same way we look to our car when we want to go shopping. There is no relationship with a person. And why? It is because of arrogance, and arrogance alone. Some folks refuse to call on the name of another human being for salvation, and so take our Lord's humanity away from Him. And for those in this group, the idea that we might call out to Jesus' Mother with the words, "Save us!" seems almost unimaginable.

But the Theotokos was a human being, just like us. A girl. Holy from her youth, to be sure, but still a human being like you and me. For those of us raised in a society steeped in the issue of rights, where political and legal structures try to make everyone equal, or try to provide opportunities that make equality possible, this seems uncomfortable. Do we really have to call out to a young single mother for salvation? Cry out most pitifully, "Most Holy Theotokos, save us"? Are we really that abject?

In a word, yes. We not only cannot save ourselves, we cannot, on our own, realize we need salvation. We can enjoy the salvation that God sends us in Jesus Christ only by admitting our complete reliance on

Him. We might neglect to honor the Theotokos because we think we can "get to" Jesus without her, but we most certainly cannot enjoy salvation without the attitude of complete submission and dependence. In his letter to the Romans, St. Paul reminds his readers that all men have received a glimpse of the glory of God in the beauty and complexity of the world around us: "For since the creation of the world His invisible attributes are clearly seen" (Romans 1:20). But how do we turn this general knowledge of the existence of God (which public polls consistently show almost everyone admits to) into genuine saving faith? We cannot, as Jesus Himself told us: "No one can come to Me unless the Father who sent Me draws him" (John 6:44). Do you see why humility is so necessary for salvation? One of the most humble acts we can perform is to sing the words, "Most Holy Theotokos, save us!" and embrace the total reliance on God that these words express.

This icon in words also contributes to our appreciation of the icons of the Theotokos that adorn our churches and homes.

Sometimes we hear icons described as "windows to heaven"—a phrase that helps the faithful to understand their unique artistic perspective in a spiritual manner. This description, however, does not apply to all icons. Look at an icon of the Last Supper. Is that a window to heaven? Are Jesus and the disciples constantly posing for that scene in heaven, with an out-of-work actor sitting in for Judas because he's not there? The same holds true for any icon representing a feastday or an event. These depict a moment in time, a moment that contributed in a grand way to the unfolding of our salvation.

It is the same with an icon of the Theotokos. She holds a baby, but that baby has grown into a man, and sits upon the throne at the right hand of God the Father. To some degree, then, an icon of the Theotokos is like a feastday icon, a commemoration of an event. But the event pictured in an icon of Mary holding the baby Jesus did not occur just once. It occurred many times, hundreds of times, thousands of times. Every time she took her child in her arms, she remembered the words of St. Simeon and St. Anna the prophetess in the temple, and she renewed herself to the task of offering her child for the salvation of the world. She remembered the words of the Archangel Gabriel, who came to announce the birth. These were sad memories for a mother, but good news for us. We need her to say "yes" to God, every day, for without that response we are lost. And so we remind her again and again, just as we shout, "Hosanna in the highest, blessed is He who comes in the name of the Lord!" before an icon of Palm Sunday, or "Christ is Risen!" before an icon of the Resurrection. In the same way, we shout, "Most Holy Theotokos, save us!" before an icon of the Virgin.

We often remember that Mary said "yes" when the angel asked her if she would become the Mother of the Savior, but we must remember that she had to raise Him from infancy as well. She had to recommit herself to her original agreement with God every day of His life as a baby, then as a toddler, then as a little boy. And remember another sacrifice she made as well, in that Jesus was her only child. Each day that she said "yes" to God, she faced the prospect of forsaking her only means of support. The half brothers of our Lord did not understand this, and brought Mary to Him while He was preaching, in order to mockingly remind Him of His responsibility to support her. She was not their mother, and they had no concern for her. They wanted Him to take care of her. Can you see her smile, can you see her renew her commitment to giving her Son for your salvation when our Lord answers, "My mother and My brothers are these who hear the word of God and do it" (Luke 8:21)? She knew, and He knew what she had given up. Some of the half brothers would never know, and some would learn only after the Resurrection, that God had come to mankind in the flesh.

The icon of the Theotokos expresses the moment of her offering her Son for our salvation. He was hers to give, just as all parents decide who can hold, care for, feed, and play with their small children. Should we wait until He's a man, and call out to Him only then, when we don't need her permission at all?

Another story from Scripture, that of the wedding at Cana in Galilee (our Scripture reading for this chapter), gives us our answer.

We normally concentrate on the miracle of the water changed into wine when we read this parable. It teaches us about the power of our Lord and gives us a kind of preamble to the rest of the Gospel. But what is the source of this miracle? I think that St. John, the author of this Gospel and this story, knew about the birth narratives in the other Gospels, and didn't want to simply repeat them. Thus he had to ask himself: What event from the life of our Lord would point to the all-important pre-eminence of His Mother, as the birth narratives do in the Gospels of St. Matthew and St. Luke? What story could St. John use from the life of Christ, something he himself had witnessed, that would show the world that Mary was the source of our salvation, not just physically (as in the one-time event of the Nativity), but continually, as she sustains a motherly relationship with her Son throughout His life, and indeed, throughout eternity? His recollection of the wedding at Cana, where she herself was the source of "this beginning of signs" (John 2:11), would provide this necessary element.

The wedding occurs early in our Lord's ministry, when Jesus had gathered His disciples around Himself but had not started teaching, preaching, healing, working miracles, or traveling. He was waiting for something, perhaps the witness of St. John the Baptist during His first trip to Jerusalem. But whatever He was waiting for, He clearly did not intend to make His powers known at the wedding. The time was not right, according to God the Father and God the Son. But the mother, the Theotokos, had different concerns. She felt for the family who couldn't afford to celebrate their children's wedding properly, for the guests who had come to wish them well, for the bride. Without wine, the celebration would end very quickly, and everyone would go home. Mary knew that her Son could help, and told Him to do so. "The lack of wine is not my concern," He told her. "We can't use the saving and miracle-working power of God to rescue a wedding celebration!"

How does the Scripture tell us Mary responded? She didn't. She's the mother, and it's not necessary for her to respond—like a bumper sticker I recently saw that said, "Because I'm your mother, that's why!" What's true today was true then. And what was true then, in terms of the influence the Theotokos has over her Divine Son, is true today.

We need help, and she possesses almost unimaginable power and influence. Should we not cry out to her, "Save us"?

Scripture Reading:
John 2:1–12

On the third day there was a wedding in Cana of Galilee, and the mother of Jesus was there. Now both Jesus and His disciples were invited to the wedding. And when they ran out of wine, the mother of Jesus said to Him, "They have no wine." Jesus said to her, "Woman, what does your concern have to do with Me? My hour has not yet come." His mother said to the servants, "Whatever He says to you, do it."

Now there were set there six waterpots of stone, according to the manner of purification of the Jews, containing twenty or thirty gallons apiece. Jesus said to them, "Fill the waterpots with water." And they filled them up to the brim. And He said to them, "Draw some out now, and take it to the master of the feast." And they took it. When the master of the feast had tasted the water that was made wine, and did not know where it came from (but the servants who had drawn the water knew), the master of the feast called the bridegroom. And he said to him, "Every man at the beginning sets out the good wine, and when the guests have well drunk, then the inferior. You have kept the good wine until now!"

This beginning of signs Jesus did in Cana of Galilee, and manifested His glory; and His disciples believed in Him.

After this He went down to Capernaum, He, His mother, His brothers, and His disciples; and they did not stay there many days.

The Theotokos continually reminds us, regarding her Son, "Do whatever He tells you."

Chapter Two

Ode One

Traversing the water as on dry land, and thereby escaping the toil of Egypt land, the Israelites cried aloud, proclaiming, "Unto our God and Redeemer, let us now sing!"

Imagine that you and I stand with other Christians in church, where we've gathered to sing the Paraklesis to the Theotokos. Our feet are still, no breeze moves the flames over the candles, the service includes no processions or entrances. We stand and sing—but in singing we journey. With the former Egyptian slaves who walked in the wilderness, escaping the *toil of Egypt*, traveling toward freedom in God's Promised Land, we walk. Can you feel with your heart the warmth of the desert sun and the ground beneath your steps?

We sing the Paraklesis *unto our God and Redeemer* because we know that in it we encounter a miracle, a miracle as historic as the parting of the Red Sea, when the Israelites *traversed the water as on dry land*. We sing the Paraklesis because we know that God loves us and helps us. God Himself, with the hosts of angels and saints that stand ever before His throne, looks down on human troubles and supplications (even your anguish and mine), and responds. God knows our lives, so we sing His praises and await His help.

Behind us, the Egyptian army rumbles. We have to escape from them, because they desire to take our life away from us. "Draw near to God and He will draw near to you" (James 4:8), the Scriptures say, and it's certainly a more comforting promise than what the world has to offer, the *toil of Egypt land*. Their chariots raise a cloud of dust only a short way behind us, and they want nothing more than for us to turn back. They're shouting that our faith is superstitious and sentimental and odd. It's the devil and his hosts, rolling their eyes at you when you go to church or pray.

And before us, suddenly, land opens where before we could see none. *Dry land.* It had been a sea, but now it looks as if water had never touched the ground at all. The army behind us sees the miracle, and their mouths drop open in unison, as if they had rehearsed the motion. On either side of the dry path, the water continues to churn, walls of sea. God has given us a way of escape! We plunge forward, and each step takes us deeper into a tunnel where water once was and still may be, and we cannot see the other side. Do you trust God enough to continue? Before us lies only the next step, and the next step, and the next. We cannot know exactly where our journey will end, but let us now sing and trust God for each footprint, trust that this journey has good things in store for us.

> *By many temptations am I distressed. In search of salvation, unto thee have I taken flight. O Mother of the Word and ever-Virgin, from ordeals and afflictions deliver me!*

Temptations distress us because they aim for nothing other than to draw us away from God. The devil doesn't care which sin you choose, as long as you choose some sin and ride it like a race car away from God's peace, forgiveness, and kingdom.

Each temptation tests us as to our willingness to follow God's law or our own will. And how distressing it is to us to find how many times we turn our backs on the One who loves us so!

But what has the Mother of God to do with our temptations? We flee to her because she gives us an example of complete obedience to the will of God. When the Archangel Gabriel came to Mary, asking her to allow God to make her the Birthgiver of His Son, what did Mary do? First she asked a question, because she wanted to understand exactly what the angel said: "How can this be, since I do not know a man?" (Luke 1:34). Then she consented to submit to the will of God. "Behold the maidservant of the Lord! Let it be to me according to your word" (1:38).

Now, having become more honorable than the cherubim, she prays for us, and helps us to find the presence of mind to turn to God in times of temptation. We seek her intercessions the same way we might seek the intercessions of anyone who is close to God, so that we might have access to all the weapons we need to battle sin.

Who can possibly describe the power of the Theotokos? Who can possibly imagine the depth of her love?

And, when we find ourselves weighed down with *ordeals and afflictions* because of our sin, the Theotokos has given us her Son. His sacrifice on the altar in heaven allows us forgiveness of sins, the only power that can destroy the power of sin and give us the salvation we search for. Sin lives in us so strongly that our desire to disobey God overcomes us constantly, even when we can see that we're destroying ourselves. Like children, we parade our independence by doing things that we know oppose the Father's will. We can see that our sin severs our relationship with God, but we continue to follow our own stubborn will. How urgently we need to know God, but what can restore the right relationship we would have had if we had avoided our constant sinning?

God Himself has the answer: He enables us to defeat sin and our sinful nature by His love. What happens to our gleeful disobedience if we're always forgiven, always loved? It loses its power and attraction. We gain nothing from it. Our independence, as a matter of fact, becomes more pronounced when we deny sin than when we embrace it. "The law of the Spirit of life in Christ Jesus has made me free from the law of sin and death" (Romans 8:2).

> *Attacks of the passions disquiet me. My soul to repletion has been filled with despondency. Bestill them, O Maiden, with the calmness of thine own Son and our God, O all-blameless one!*

The attack comes without warning, and you have no time to think. You cannot see the attack with your eyes, because it occurs underneath your skin, inside you. You, yourself, are the enemy. What could be more *disquieting* than this predicament, or could cause us more to cry out to the Theotokos for help and *calm*?

Sadly, many things. Because of our selfishness, there are many things in our lives that disquiet us more than our sin: fear of the future, difficult people, money troubles, political problems, illness, mental anguish.

It is this tendency—the habit of concerning ourselves with many problems other than our own sins—that makes our situation so horrific. We're comfortable with our own sins, but the sins of others bother us like a bad rash! Thus, when we pray the words, *My soul to repletion has been filled with despondency*, most of us have to pray them as a supplication, as if to say, "Make my soul sorry for its sin." We are forced to ask God to fill our souls to their fullness with despair for the sin that our passions cause ("Attacks of the passions, disquiet me!"). Otherwise, without God's help, we may miss the whole point of the spiritual life, which is to overcome sin and gain peace with God. When we pray the Paraklesis to the Theotokos, we pray it to sensitize ourselves to that despair we should have, even more than to express the despair we actually have. We pray that God would make us sensitive to sin.

This kind of prayer has a long tradition in the Christian faith. Thousands before you have prayed for agitation of soul, for sensitivity to sin, and for God to show them where they have disappointed Him. In the prayers of thanksgiving after Holy Communion, we pray, "And grant unto me tears of repentance and confession, that I may hymn Thee and glorify Thee all the days of my life." When agitation comes, when godly sorrow becomes a part of your spiritual repertoire, you know that spiritual maturity cannot be far off. "For godly sorrow produces repentance leading to salvation, not to be regretted" (2 Corinthians 7:10).

It's distressing to a spiritual father when his spiritual children come to confession and have no sins to confess. It means that they have no sensitivity to sin at all. "Are you perfect?" I sometimes ask when I run into a situation like this.

Everyone answers this question the same way: "No, I am not perfect."

"In what ways are you not perfect?" I ask. "What are your sins?" I try to open some doors, to introduce to the person the possibility of sensitivity to sin.

Usually I get the same reply: "Oh, I don't know." So I have to urge the person to pray that God would show him his sins. Pray for sadness, I tell him, pray for anguish over your sins. It's difficult to tell someone that I wish he were a little more unhappy!

The fathers call this "joy-producing sorrow." And St. Paul speaks of it as well: "For godly sorrow produces repentance leading to salvation, not to be regretted. . . . For observe this very thing, that you sorrowed in a godly manner: What diligence it produced in you, what clearing of yourselves, what indignation, what fear, what vehement desire, what zeal, what vindication!" (2 Corinthians 7:10–11).

> *To God and the Savior thou gavest birth. I beg thee, O Virgin, from afflictions deliver me. For now unto thee I flee for refuge, bringing to thee both my soul and my reasoning!*

What can we say about someone who gave birth to God? We know from Scripture and from the Creed that God existed before time, and yet He has a mother. How can that be? How can we possibly express our love for her and thanks to her for giving us our salvation, not as a philosophy, a law, a book, or a ceremony, but as a baby?

What can we say about someone who gave birth to God? I know that we can say that we want to *flee* to her *for refuge*, we want to know her and know about her, to consider the miracle of her birthgiving and of her motherhood. She gave my Savior the blood by which I am redeemed. "In Him we have redemption through His blood, the forgiveness of sins" (Ephesians 1:7). She held Him in her arms, and fed Him from herself. What can we say? Any words that come to mind might be better sung than spoken, for they come as much from our *souls* as from our *reasoning*.

This ode gives us pause to consider one of the great paradoxes of the Christian faith. When we pray, we often ask for something to be better in our lives; we ask for more comfort and less suffering. Is this a good reason to sing the Paraklesis, the supplicatory canon to the Theotokos? Consider these scripture passages: "[We are] heirs of God and joint heirs with Christ, if indeed we suffer with Him, that we may also be glorified together" (Romans 8:17). "In everything give thanks; for this is the will of God in Christ Jesus for you" (1 Thessalonians 5:18). Didn't Jesus say to the sons of Zebedee that they would indeed have to suffer as He did, with no promise of earthly glory in return (Matthew 20:20–23)? In these passages, the Scripture seems to imply that God cannot save us without first allowing us to suffer.

Yet, we plead with the Theotokos to deliver us from afflictions, and we often pray to God to improve, or help us improve, our circumstances. And in this we have the example of our Lord, who healed many people in the Gospels. Why would He heal people if suffering were necessary for salvation? Why didn't He simply talk to them, teach them, help them put their suffering in a proper perspective? But He reduced their sufferings and gave them comfort. We have all experienced comfort-giving answers to our prayers. So how do we accept the Scripture's call to suffer, and pray for deliverance at the same time?

First, we must understand the healings of Scripture as parables in action. Of course, all Christians believe that the miracles of Scripture actually took place, that real physical changes happened in the people Christ touched and for whom He prayed, and that healings have occurred in His Name throughout history. But it's also important to see the healings in the light of Jesus' whole ministry: He spoke with authority not only because He spoke the truth, but because the people saw His miracles. The miracles made them listen, and then some of them who listened actually understood and followed Christ for eternal salvation, irrespective of the miracles. But the miracles didn't just advertise the gospel, as if Christ had blown a big trumpet before making an important announcement. The miracles of healing and exorcism told the people that God loved them, that He wanted (and wants today) to bring people to Himself, who contains the fullness of life. The miracles point to the ultimate will of God, which is eternal life and joy.

And these miracle/parables still occur. Just as the reality of the spoken parables didn't stop just because Christ had communicated the deeper meaning behind them, so the reality of the parables in action continues as well. Mustard seeds still grow, they still start out small and grow very large, just as Jesus said. Likewise, Jesus and faith in Him still heals human beings and releases them from spiritual bondage. Even today, He performs miracles of healing and comfort. But we must accept them the same way the first followers of our Lord understood them—as signposts pointing to Him, and not as ends in themselves. "Then some of the scribes and Pharisees answered, saying, 'Teacher, we want to see a sign from You.' But He answered and said to them, 'An evil and adulterous generation seeks after a sign, and no sign will be given to it. . . .'" (Matthew 12:38–39).

Secondly, we must understand the difference between accepting suffering and contenting ourselves with suffering. When St. Paul had a physical problem of some kind, he prayed fervently that God would take it away from him (2 Corinthians 12:7–9). We do not seek suffering because we like it. We don't long to be uncomfortable, or pray for sickness and disease. We pray to be spared from them: "Do not lead us into temptation" (Luke 11:4). But when trials come to us, and we pray to be delivered, but the trials remain, then we know that God has called us to the same ministry to which He called St. Paul. Our Lord revealed that His "strength is made perfect in weakness" (2 Corinthians 12:9), that followers of Christ will suffer in this world as their Lord suffered. It's a part of God's redeeming work, and accepting it is a ministry in itself.

> *Diseased are my body and my soul. Do thou make me worthy of divine guidance and thy care, O thou who alone art God's Mother, for thou art good and the Birthgiver of the good!*

How is my *body diseased?* It is diseased when I don't eat for just one short day, or even part of one day, and I feel it pleading for food as if it's being starved. My body is diseased when it demands that I forsake the love of the next world for the love of feeding it with comfort and pleasure in this one. I'm diseased when I long for heat and water and comfort and satisfaction even more than I long for God.

For this reason the Paraklesis tells you that your body contains disease, and that you should look to the words as a welcome reminder of your real condition. You are diseased. Your body lives only for comfort and spreads its disease to your soul, which is weakened by the body's relentless complaining, and often simply gives the body what it wants. Thus, the body diseases the soul. At birth, the inclination to sin fills our souls, but the actual sin enters us when we allow ourselves to be controlled by those inclinations: "Beloved, I beg you as sojourners and pilgrims, abstain from fleshly lusts which war against the soul" (1 Peter 2:11). What does he mean by "fleshly lusts"? These words sound too lurid to apply to most of us, but they really refer to any of the numerous ways in which we coddle our bodies while starving our souls.

Make me worthy of divine guidance, we sing to the Theotokos. Our sickness debilitates us, but rather than asking for healing, we wisely ask for guidance.

Scripture Reading:
Luke 1:26–38

Now in the sixth month the angel Gabriel was sent by God to a city of Galilee named Nazareth, to a virgin betrothed to a man whose name was Joseph, of the house of David. The virgin's name was Mary. And having come in, the angel said to her, "Rejoice, highly favored one, the Lord is with you; blessed are you among women!"

But when she saw him, she was troubled at his saying, and considered what manner of greeting this was. Then the angel said to her, "Do not be afraid, Mary, for you have found favor with God. And behold, you will conceive in your womb and bring forth a Son, and shall call His name Jesus. He will be great, and will be called the Son of the Highest; and the Lord God will give Him the throne of His father David. And He will reign over the house of Jacob forever, and of His kingdom there will be no end."

Then Mary said to the angel, "How can this be, since I do not know a man?"

And the angel answered and said to her, "The Holy Spirit will come upon you, and the power of the Highest will overshadow you; therefore, also, that Holy One who is to be born will be called the Son of God. Now indeed, Elizabeth your relative has also conceived a son in her old age; and this is now the sixth month for her who was called barren. For with God nothing will be impossible."

Then Mary said, "Behold the maidservant of the Lord! Let it be to me according to your word." And the angel departed from her.

In the Annunciation, God comes to Mary through the mediation of an angel to ask for her permission to make her the Mother of His Son. We can see in this passage the familiarity she had with spiritual things, her consideration of God's request, and her agreement with the will of God.

Chapter Three

Ode Three

Of the vault of the heavens art Thou, O Lord, fashioner. So too of the church art Thou founder—do Thou establish me in unfeigned love for Thee, who art the height of things sought for and staff of the faithful, O Thou only friend of man!

Our Lord fashioned *the vault of the heavens:* "by Him all things were created that are in heaven and that are on earth" (Colossians 1:16), and also He is *the founder of the Church:* "He is the head of the body, the church, who is the beginning, the firstborn from the dead" (Colossians 1:18). He created them the same way—by the word of His Spirit. The earth and heavens were created as described in the scriptural Book of Genesis (Genesis 1:1), and the Church by His Holy Spirit on Pentecost (Acts 2:1–4). God has continued to sustain both. But while St. Peter tells us the heavens and earth will eventually be transformed, "the heavens will pass away with a great noise, and the elements will melt with fervent heat; both the earth and the works that are in it will be burned up" (2 Peter 3:10), St. Matthew reminds us that the Church will never pass away: "And I say to you that you are Peter, and on this rock I will build My church, and the gates of Hades shall not prevail against it" (Matthew 16:18).

We may look at particular local churches and wonder if and when they will pass away, or wonder how they survive at all, the same way we see trees full of life in the summer creaking like empty sticks in the winter. But after we live some years and come to expect the changing of the seasons, we realize that the dead winter world has not died at all. What appears to have died comes to life again in the spring. So it is with the Church. When we look from an eternal perspective, we readily agree that it will never perish.

We experience the eternal nature of the Church in the Divine Liturgy. The Liturgy brings all that has ever been, all that shall ever be, and all places into one place, into the Holy Church of God, where God-minded people gather to worship Him and bless His eternal Kingdom. God the Creator, One in Three, speaks to His children through their prayers and praises, and through His words spoken in the Scriptures. What greater blessing can we imagine? What simplicity? You don't need to look for God here and there—you can see Him in His Church. You don't need to listen for news here and there of a miracle or a new teaching, because all that you need dwells eternally and completely in the fullness of the Church. What greater blessing can there be in this world, what more obvious evidence of the Church's eternal nature?

We need only to look to the treasure we have in the Church and we find ourselves established in the love of God. When we seek Him in fasting and prayer, we discover that He is indeed the *Friend* above all friends. Our enemy, the devil, lures us into a hateful dependence on himself by filling us with longing for comfort, security, and pleasure. But God calls us to a real friendship, built of trust and purity. We cherish our longing when our longing is for Him. It has no satisfaction in this world. To find out for yourself, stand in the church. Sing to Him. Seek the heights where He dwells. Your longing for Him becomes your staff and support. You spring from grace to grace, allowing God to satisfy you with Himself.

What greater joy is there? None.

> *I have thee as the shelter and the defense of my life—thou the God-birthgiver and Virgin, pilot and govern me into thy sheltered port; for thou art author of good things and staff of the faithful, O thou only lauded one!*

In the same way the Theotokos walked, we must walk. We find the footprints of her passage in Scripture, in the great traditions of the Church, and in our hearts. We must place our feet exactly into those prints. Sometimes the way is easy and joyful, and sometimes a sword pierces our hearts. In difficult times we need refuge and help, but where to find it? Where did the Mother of God find refuge and help? The Scriptures tell us, "Lord, Thou hast been our refuge in generation and generation" (Psalm 89). The Theotokos continually sought shelter in God. And who was the defense of the Mother of God during her difficult years on earth? Again, the Scriptures say, "As for me, unto God have I cried, and the Lord hearkened unto me" (Psalm 54). The answer, again, is God Himself. How often we seek to take onto ourselves the cares and responsibilities that belong to God alone! He provides us with shelter, and He defends us, and He has given us the *God-birthgiver and Virgin* as *pilot and author of good things.* The path of her steps leads us toward the comfort and peace that God has to give.

This simple way of life, in which you leave to God the matters that belong to Him and only accept the cares that belong to yourself, is very difficult to sustain. From our earliest years, adults have taught us to worry about the future. We brush our teeth, study hard, eat properly, and save money, not in order to keep ourselves clean and bright, but because we want to avoid what will happen if we don't—even if we don't know what that fearsome consequence might be.

I used to visit a very old woman who lived by herself. She constantly cleaned her house, over and over, day after day. As soon as she finished she started again. She would often miss church, supposedly in order to clean on Sunday mornings.

"Why do you worry so much about cleaning?" I asked her.

"What if someone comes, do I want them to see a dirty house?" But no one ever came to visit her—I was the only one. Was it for me that she cleaned and cleaned and cleaned? I'm not sure, but I wish she had cleaned less and attended to the worship of God more.

When we worry about the future, our spirits become burdened and we run from task to task to task in order to make sure that we prepare ourselves for whatever might come. But is this possible? We know in the backs of our minds that we cannot prepare for everything, and that we have most likely left something important undone. We're not sure what this important thing might be, and so we let the nagging feeling of dread snore away in the back of our heads.

It's very difficult for us to change except when we seek shelter in the Holy Mother of God and in her Son. Jesus said, "Therefore I say to you, do not worry about your life" (Matthew 6:25). The Theotokos had one child and one betrothed. Joseph died while Jesus was still young, and God called her to give up her Son for the salvation of the world. From where then would come her sustenance, her support, her protection? Who would watch over her in her old age? God and God alone. She embodied her Son's advice to His followers, "But seek first the kingdom of God and His righteousness, and all these things shall be added to you" (Matthew 6:33).

I have thee as the shelter and the defense of my life, we sing to her. And as we do, we pray that we can have the same peace that she had, to walk in the same way she walked, and that like her we can seek God's righteousness above all things.

> *I beseech thee, O Virgin, do thou dispel far from me all of the distress of despair and turbulence in my soul. For thou, O Bride of God, hast given birth to the Lord Christ, who is the Prince of peace, O thou the all-blameless one.*

In this verse, we cry out to God that our souls are *distressed* and *turbulent,* because of *despair.* Ah, despair! The disease of our time, of all times, of our generation and all generations. Why is despair so widespread and so popular? Because it is born in self-love.

I can say that despair is the result of self-love in print more easily than I can say it to a person's face. When I'm facing a depressed and desperate person, I try to teach them that their discomfort comes from an abundance of self-love if, and only if, I have a very close relationship with that person. Otherwise, my words seem harsh and ridiculous and the person cannot hear them at all.

But it's true. Despair and depression spring from self-love, and from no place else. A person says to himself, "I don't deserve the life I'm getting. I deserve better. I'm a better person than thousands of people who have better lives, is that fair?" Indeed, the concept of fairness leads us to despair, because life on earth is not fair, and when we expect to find fairness in life, our expectation always disappoints us.

Life is not fair, because we benefit not only from our own worthiness, but from the worthiness of the generations that have gone before us. All the forebears of my nation, my community, my family, the church I belong to, and schools I attend have contributed to the wonderful life

I have. Is that fair? No, not at all, but it's right. It's right that those people took the responsibility to sacrifice something of their own lives to make the future better for their children, grandchildren, and so on. And in addition, it's right that I have the opportunity, as they did, to make life better for those who will come after me. Why isn't this fair? It's not fair because it means that someone else who lives in a country, a community, a family where those who came before didn't or couldn't think about the generations to come, or were not able for whatever reason to make the world a better place for unborn generations, does not have the opportunities and good life that I have. Should my life be taken from me and given to that person in the name of fairness? Some might think so, but they think this based on their own self-love. "I want what you have," they say, or worse yet, "Everyone should have what you have," and they become desperate because this cannot be.

So what do I have to do in order to benefit from the good things that my ancestors have given me? I only need to be born. In one place, a child is born to a wealthy and happy family, another is born to a poor and unhappy family, and still another is killed by his mother before he could be born at all.

This *distresses* us, and leads some to *despair*. What can we do about the unfairness of this life? Look not at the glory of this fallen world, but instead see the gift that everyone has, the gift that puts unfairness in its place. That is the gift of Jesus Christ. This is more than a "pie in the sky" false comfort. Christ saves us from sin and death. What else can do that? Does money, or a happy home, or school? He gives us the unfailing promise of the heavenly kingdom. "For the wages of sin is death, but the free gift of God is eternal life in Christ Jesus our Lord" (Romans 6:23). He is the *Prince of peace*, the Son of Mary.

> *Since thou barest our good's cause and our Benefactor too, from the wealth of thy lovingkindness do thou pour forth on all. For thou canst do all things, being one mighty in power, for thou didst bring forth Christ. O blessed of God art thou!*

How can the one who has given us the Christ as Savior not long to give us *all things*? And what things exist that she cannot give, or refuses to give? Only those things that do not serve our good, those things that do not lead us to salvation, these are the things that the *one mighty in power* keeps back from her children. The Mother of God knows me, she knows me by name, and desires above all things that I might accept the *wealth of her lovingkindness*, which is in her gift of Christ Himself.

We understand the wealth and power of the Mother of God when we remember that she gave her Son to us as her gift to the world. After the Spirit-filled Simeon blessed the Lord at the sight of the Child Jesus in the temple, he blessed the Lord's parents and said to Mary His Mother, "Behold, this Child is destined for the fall and rising of many in Israel, and for a sign which will be spoken against (yes, a sword will pierce through your own soul also)" (Luke 2:34–35a). She bore the Benefactor, she brought Him forth, and it was up to her whether she would give Him over to the prophecies she had heard, or keep Him for herself. It was, in a way of speaking, her right. It all depended on her will, on her decision. Did she love the world enough to give up her Son, or would she leave the place where the Archangel came to her and never speak to anyone of that day again? So, the power of the Theotokos does not rest in physical or intellectual strength, in artistic ability or the loyalty of her followers. Rather, her wealth is her lovingkindness, her will, her "yes" to God.

In this way, we all become like the Mother of God. The fallen world seeks to force us to make certain decisions, and even deviously uses our free will to lead us away from God. Some people think they exercise freedom when they do whatever they want. These people fill drug and alcohol rehabs, counseling centers, hospitals, courts, and jails. Is that freedom?

We become free when we say "yes" to God as the Theotokos did, and when we decide to give our suffering, our hopes, even our very lives to Him for the sake of the world.

With most grievous diseases and with corrupt passions, too, I am put to trial, O Virgin. Come thou unto my aid, for I know thee to be an inexhaustible treasure of unfailing healing, O thou, the all-blameless one.

Once when Jesus was teaching in Capernaum, when He had been away for some time and the people had waited anxiously to see Him return, the house was so crowded that a certain little band of men, bearing their friend prone on a stretcher, could not even get near the door to go in and ask our Lord to heal the one they carried. They went up on the roof and took tiles off so that the sun fell into the crowded room in straight, bright lines, and lowering their friend down like a prophet descending from heaven itself, they left him dangling in the air in front of the face of God Incarnate (Mark 2:1–12).

Jesus healed the man, but He healed him by telling him that his sins were forgiven. The crowd sitting at His feet was shocked. Would there be no sacrifice, prayers, or pilgrimage? Just one man saying to another, "Your sins are forgiven"? This was, to them, an outrage. They had no problem with Jesus healing people who needed healing, but they could not accept that He would forgive them their sins.

Jesus knew what they thought of His words and asked them, "Which is easier, to say to the paralytic, 'Your sins are forgiven you,' or to say, 'Arise, take up your bed and walk'?" (Mark 2:9). What could He mean, other than that the healing of our souls and the healing of our bodies are essentially the same? Certainly, Jesus was not giving His listeners a lesson in grammar, but a spiritual truth: The disease and the healing of the soul influences the disease and healing of the body. They are connected.

It is this connection that puts us to trial. We are put to trial because we fail to believe that we deserve all the suffering we encounter. When I suffer, I complain, and this complaining is a passion that draws me further and further away from the healing hand of God. When I suffer, I fail to see that my sin has kept me from the joy of knowing God, and I only think about the deterioration of my earthly body. It is in this that the Theotokos offers healing. She prays for us, that we might understand the reality of disease, and the passions, and healing. And she provides for us a model of patience while suffering, of humility, that gives us hope and grace.

Scripture Reading:

I Samuel 2:1–11

And Hannah prayed and said:

"My heart rejoices in the LORD;

My horn is exalted in the LORD.

I smile at my enemies,

Because I rejoice in Your salvation.

No one is holy like the LORD,

For there is none besides You,

Nor is there any rock like our God.

Talk no more so very proudly;

Let no arrogance come from your mouth,

For the LORD is the God of knowledge;

And by Him actions are weighed.

The bows of the mighty men are broken,

And those who stumbled are girded with strength.

Those who were full have hired themselves out for bread,

And the hungry have ceased to hunger.

Even the barren has borne seven,

And she who has many children has become feeble.

The LORD kills and makes alive;

He brings down to the grave and brings up.

The LORD makes poor and makes rich;

He brings low and lifts up.

He raises the poor from the dust

And lifts the beggar from the ash heap,

To set them among princes

And make them inherit the throne of glory.

For the pillars of the earth are the LORD's,

And He has set the world upon them.

He will guard the feet of His saints,

But the wicked shall be silent in darkness.

For by strength no man shall prevail.

The adversaries of the Lord shall be broken in pieces;

From heaven He will thunder against them.

The Lord will judge the ends of the earth.

He will give strength to His king,

And exalt the horn of His anointed."

Then Elkanah went to his house at Ramah. But the child ministered to the LORD

before Eli the priest.

Luke 1:46–56

And Mary said:

"My soul magnifies the Lord,

And my spirit has rejoiced in God my Savior.

For He has regarded the lowly state of His maidservant;

For behold, henceforth all generations will call me blessed.

For He who is mighty has done great things for me,

And holy is His name.

And His mercy is on those who fear Him

From generation to generation.

He has shown strength with His arm;

He has scattered the proud in the imagination of their hearts.

He has put down the mighty from their thrones,

And exalted the lowly.

He has filled the hungry with good things,

And the rich He has sent away empty.

He has helped His servant Israel,

In remembrance of His mercy,

As He spoke to our fathers,

To Abraham and to his seed forever."

And Mary remained with her about three months, and returned to her house.

Compare the songs of Hannah and Mary. They both speak of the awesome power of God, of His love for the humble and poor, and of His protection of the faithful. But notice one difference: the Holy Spirit says through Mary that "all generations shall call [her] blessed" (v. 48). The Theotokos tells us in the Scriptures that she must be remembered and blessed by all who call themselves Christian.

Chapter Four

Troparion between Odes Three and Four

O fervent advocate, invincible battlement, fountain of mercy and sheltering retreat for the world—earnestly we cry to thee, Lady, Mother of God, hasten and save us from all imperilment, for thou alone art our speedy protectress!

Now we pause to consider the troparion that introduces the next section of the Paraklesis. This little hymn gives seven names to Mary, names meant to inspire and encourage us, teach us, fill us, and draw us closer to God and to the Mother who bore the second Person of the One and Triune Divinity.

Fervent Advocate: Saints offer us two benefits, and the first is that their lives teach us about the ways of God. When we see their sacrifice, their holiness and wisdom, we see what we might become. Their writings beckon us to a higher life, and if they have no writings, the things written about them do the same. They teach us the very limits of the scriptural statement: "I have been crucified with Christ; it is no longer I who live, but Christ lives in me" (Galatians 2:20). This leads us to ask ourselves: How far did the saints take this new life, and can I also make my own life into the holy thing that God has intended it to be?

The life of the Theotokos, more than that of any other saint, gives us a model of the spiritual heights to which a human can aspire. I surprised a young man one time when I invited him to our church with the promise that we have hanging throughout the building pictures of gorgeous models. He came, and I saw him looking all around during and after the liturgy. I went and asked him if he'd noticed the models, and he smiled nervously—I think he wondered if I was crazy. As we spoke, we stood next to an icon of the Theotokos. "Here's one," I said, "the most lovely of supermodels, the most beautiful and the highest expression of humanity." He laughed, amused, but also listened intently as I tried to describe to him how she did indeed live the most lovely and liberated of lives.

The second benefit of the saints is their intercession for us. If we only see the saints as models, then we forget that they are alive even now, standing eternally before the throne of God, praying for those they love, for those who love them and plead for their help. We express this truth in regard to the Theotokos when we call her *Fervent Advocate*. Whom could we ask to pray for us with any more influence over God than His Mother? Not only does she offer prayers for us, but she does so fervently and with strength. She longs above all things to make use of her power for our benefit. "Most Holy Theotokos, save us!" we cry, and she hears us and responds to our love for her and our belief that she can do all things.

Invincible Battlement: There are times when we make direct attacks upon the kingdom of Satan. Sometimes on my knees, sometimes on my soapbox I turn my attention toward the bad things I see and try to make them right. I turn on my computer, or pick up the phone, or open my checkbook and try as best I can to make the world a better place.

But there are other times, times I'm not so proud of, when the enemy of souls has me on the run. I get tired or discouraged, or I feel alone in what I suppose is my love for God, and I can almost hear Satan laugh and see him smile. I need to retreat, but to where? What fortress do Christians have, and to what battlement can we run? Certainly, our lives are hidden in Christ, and it is to Him that we run for salvation. But to what motherly presence do we run like children suddenly aware of the dangerous nature of the world, afraid and perhaps wounded in a great and desperate battle? We run to the Theotokos, our refuge and help. Even the martyrs, who did not enjoy any respite in this world, looked to her for their strength. They now dwell with her and her Son eternally in the eternal invincible battlement.

Fountain of Mercy: I am constantly amazed at the mercy of God. I go to confession four times each year to my spiritual father, who lives some distance from my home. I find myself trying to think of something different to say each time I go. The same sins defeat me again and again, but do I want to repeat these same sins to my spiritual father every time I go? I often do, but I'm always worried that either he or God will grow tired of hearing the same confessions so many times. This is why I think it's so hard for many people to attend to the sacrament of confession year after year—they have nothing new to say and are ashamed to say the same things time and time again. Does God's patience have a limit? The Bible mentions that we should forgive sins even unto seventy times seven. That's 490. Have I overeaten 490 times, or been unnecessarily angry, or greedy? Have I heard over 490 words of gossip, or spoken as many? Have 490 days passed when I didn't take a proper amount of time to pray? Certainly, the Scripture does not speak literally here, as if we should keep track of how many times a certain person has done something needing forgiveness so that we can stop precisely at the 490th one. (How would any marriage survive?) Even so, I find myself irrationally worrying that God might say, "All right, the fact that you continue to sin in this way tells me that you really do not love Me at all; in fact, it shows that you love no one but yourself. I can no longer forgive that particular sin."

But I have no need to worry. Can we exhaust the mercy of God? Not at all. Even if you spend as much time as possible deliberately sinning in a particular way, so as to try to overcome God's mercy, it won't happen. The only thing that stops the flow is when you stop going to the fountain. The Theotokos is a *fountain of mercy*, she continually intercedes for you, in spite of all that you've done and all that you continue to do. But she is like any fountain, in one particular place and not in all places. A fountain that covers the world is not a fountain but a flood, a destructive thing. A fountain that continually flows forth mercy contains itself, awaiting your repentance, sorrow, and genuine desire to love God in all things. Go there.

Sheltering Retreat for the World: I find myself singing this part of the hymn two different ways: sheltering retreat *from* the world, and sheltering retreat *for* the world. I think that if the original of the hymn had read "from" the world, I wouldn't have sung anything different. But there are times when I sing this troparion that I cannot possibly imagine that the Theotokos is a retreat *for* the whole world, and that's why I think I misspeak it now and then. I look at the lives of some people, what they like and how they spend their time and money, and I want to get away from them, to keep the Church hidden from them. It's selfish of me to say this, but I'm being honest.

For instance, one August I arrived at my church to prepare for the small group of people who would come to sing the Paraklesis, and across the street our neighborhood welfare mom was fighting with her latest male friend. Their screaming and cursing filled the lovely summer evening. I paused outside the church to watch them, not because I enjoyed watching them argue, but so that I could call the police if the two of them started pummeling one another with more than words. After awhile the man looked like he'd had enough and started toward his car, but the woman followed, escalating her attacks and threats, and he stopped. He hissed something I couldn't hear, and although I could not have imagined that she could shout louder and say more filthy things to him than she already had, she did. I could distinguish her words as English, but I didn't understand one word of what she was saying. Well, truthfully, I understood one of her words, one clear word that she said over and over again. Not that I wanted to understand anything else she was saying. Inside the house, the TV blared downstairs and a stereo thudded forth a ribcage-quaking deluge of rap music, or something like it, upstairs. Her children, it seemed, didn't want to hear what she was saying any more than I did.

As I walked into the church to reverence the icons, I asked myself, is this the world *to* which I have been called? Or *out of* which I have been called? The answer, of course, is both. The woman's voice continued to flow in through the open windows of the church, and the sound grotesquely floated over the peaceful icons. Normally, our choir would fill that space with beautiful and harmonious music, but as I stood before the altar hearing our neighbor scream and curse, the choir members were absent and a filthy sound filled the entire church.

I can only escape the world, I remind myself, by living the life I was given in Jesus Christ at my baptism. But it doesn't mean that I can turn my back on those who haven't. I can't possibly, in good conscience, keep the Church hidden from anyone. Even the monastic in a secluded place makes the bitter evil of the world his companion as he struggles to make himself a worthy intercessor for all people. The Theotokos calls all to herself, all to the forgiveness and new life in her Son. She is the *sheltering retreat* from the world *for the world*.

Lady: Feminists don't like this word, because it denotes a certain propriety and loveliness that they eschew. It's the female equivalent of the word "gentleman," a chivalrous word that denotes respect for women, protection, and selflessness. I suppose this angers those who believe that women do not need the protection of men, nor their concern. I cannot imagine what the world would be like if men did not have a concern for and protective attitude toward women; certainly it would not be a better place than it is. But when we call the Theotokos "lady," what does the expression bring about in us, what does it suggest to us about ourselves in reference to the Mother of God?

This brings to mind a man who served as the Sunday school superintendent in our church when I was growing up, an older retired man who served in this position for many years. To my friends and me (we were a handful), the Sunday school had all the fun of regular school without any of the hard work. We had great—and very patient—Sunday school teachers in our church. But the Sunday school superintendent was a little different. Whenever he came around, we straightened up. He embodied all the seriousness of the faith, all the depth and power of the Scriptures, and the lofty nature of the Christian's calling. He was not fun; nice, but not fun. He never punished us or yelled at us or even threatened us, but when he spoke, we all shut our mouths and listened. If we were fooling around, and we saw him, we stopped. It wasn't that we were afraid of him as much as that he embodied all the maturity and honorable qualities that we hoped to grow into someday, and we felt (and therefore acted) more mature in his presence.

This is the effect of the word "lady." When I say it, I call into mind the presence of one who has lived the most honorable of lives. She did all things properly, patiently, seriously. Perhaps some people reject the memory of the Theotokos because she brings this element into the spirituality of the Christian faith. She is not here for fun. She is here to show you, especially at those times when you need to be reminded, that God calls you to be a distinguished and respectable citizen of His kingdom and of this world.

Mother of God: Ultimately, this name for Mary sums up all we deem to be important about her. This is why there are so few icons depicting the Theotokos without her Child, because it's the child that makes the mother.

I had an old friend who asked to visit me at the beginning of one particular August, and I told him that he was very welcome to stay at our house, but that each night of his visit I would have to go to church and lead the Paraklesis. He was not an Orthodox Christian. "What's a Paraklesis?" he asked me.

"It's a long series of hymns to the Mother of God," I answered.

"The Mother of God! I can't imagine that God has a mother!" To his Protestant ears, these words seemed outrageous.

"Well, let me ask you something. Is Jesus God?" I asked him.

"Yes, Jesus is God the Incarnate Son."

"Is Mary His Mother?"

"Of course."

"Then in what way is Mary not the Mother of God? To deny it is to say one of two things: either Jesus is not God, or Mary is not His Mother."

My friend paused, thinking about what I had said. "Mother of God. It just sounds funny."

Indeed. It sounds funny, in an odd, not a humorous, way. How can God have a mother? A mother naturally must exist before her child, but no human ever existed before God, because nothing has ever existed that can be called "before God." It's equally difficult to imagine that God could choose to come to the world as a baby, the same way that all babies come into the world. But He did, He lowered Himself to our state, and to our pattern of existence. What marvelous condescension! So we see that the term *Mother of God*, when applied to Mary, must necessarily follow from the miracle of the Incarnation. But it does not only follow from the Incarnation, it also teaches us about the Incarnation, which is the astounding miracle that Jesus came to this world to save us.

Speedy Protectress: She is the Mother of God and an invincible battlement. But in addition, we need only close our eyes and pray, and she stands beside us, listening. "O *Mother of God*, my protection, *save me* from this *imperilment*, from this danger I see before me." She hears, and quickly, she helps.

Scripture Reading:
Genesis 28:11–17
So he came to a certain place and stayed there all night, because the sun had set. And he took one of the stones of that place and put it at his head, and he lay

down in that place to sleep. Then he dreamed, and behold, a ladder was set up on the earth, and its top reached to heaven; and there the angels of God were ascending and descending on it.

And behold, the LORD stood above it and said: "I am the LORD God of Abraham your father and the God of Isaac; the land on which you lie I will give to you and your descendants. Also your descendants shall be as the dust of the earth; you shall spread abroad to the west and the east, to the north and the south; and in you and in your seed all the families of the earth shall be blessed. Behold, I am with you and will keep you wherever you go, and will bring you back to this land; for I will not leave you until I have done what I have spoken to you."

Then Jacob awoke from his sleep and said, "Surely the LORD is in this place, and I did not know it." And he was afraid and said, "How awesome is this place! This is none other than the house of God, and this is the gate of heaven!"

In his dream of a ladder stretching from heaven to earth, Jacob beholds the unseen reality of the spiritual world (really, for the first time in his life), a world which exists all around him even when he is not aware of it.

The Theotokos is also described as a ladder linking the earth to heaven. Often, we are not aware that she works continually in our lives to help us on the path toward salvation. But even without any miraculous dreams, we can enjoy the same insights that Jacob had: that the unseen is real, that there is a link from earth to heaven, and that we have one who loves us and calls us to a closer relationship with God.

Chapter Five

Ode Four

I have hearkened and heard, O Lord, of Thy dispensations' most awesome mystery, and I came to knowledge of Thy works, and I sang the praise of Thy Divinity.

Can you see the progression in this verse—from hearing, to knowing, to singing? This progression describes the work of God's grace in our lives, a work of cooperation between ourselves and God.

Our Lord forces Himself on no one. Even if you received the sacrament of baptism as an infant and had no choice in the matter, it is still true that at some point in your life you must make (or have made) the decision to live the life in Christ your baptism gave you. The Holy Spirit either lives in you, a gift from the Church and from your godparents, or calls you to Christ if you are not baptized. Either way, you cannot gain more of God's grace without your own willing determination to embrace Him.

This process starts as a gift from God, when He gives a measure of His grace to every human being: "For since the creation of the world His invisible attributes are clearly seen, being understood by the things that are made, even His eternal power and Godhead, so that they are without excuse" (Romans 1:20). This is the "hearing" part of the verse above. We hear from someone that God exists, and something resonates in our hearts with the truth of this statement, and we realize that God's existence has something to do with us. But it's something we don't know fully, only something we've *hearkened* to *and heard*.

Then after this initial revelation of grace, if we turn to God in any way and at any level, God responds with another level, a further measure of His grace. With each response on our part to the gift comes

another, greater gift: "Draw near to God and He will draw near to you
. . . Humble yourselves in the sight of the Lord, and He will lift you up"
(James 4:8, 10). This is the *knowledge* level of the verse above. Perhaps
you are not yet intimate with God, but you have started to know things
about Him, you start learning the Truth of God.

Your relationship to God is the same as your relationship with any
other person. When you first meet someone, you may spend a few
moments, or perhaps hours, speaking together. But you maintain some
kind of distance and hold some things back. Then after some further
encounters, some additional time together, you become more acquainted
and share more of yourselves with one another. The person may become more than an acquaintance, may become a friend. And how do
you reach this point? Time and attention. You reach that point by spending time getting to know the person.

And then there are some people, perhaps only one or two in your
whole life, with whom you share a very deep relationship, a relationship
of almost total sharing and openness. And many find a spouse who
becomes almost like the other half of the one person the two of you
comprise.

It's the same with the Divine Person, God. After you hear about
God, then learn about God, you begin to sing about God: *and I sang the
praise of Thy divinity*. You've spent good time together, and have told
each other about yourselves. You become rather fond of one another,
and your relationship has grown deep and rich. You talk often together
and every word is a joy.

Remember the story of Paul and Silas and the Philippian jailer?
When he received the apostles into his prison, the jailer "fastened their
feet in the stocks" (Acts 16:24). This incarceration was incredibly painful and uncomfortable, and the jailers often left prisoners in the stocks
not just overnight, but for even days and weeks at a time. Can you
imagine this scene? Your back against a wall and your legs stretched out
in front of you, pulled wide apart and fastened to the floor? But listen
how the apostles reacted to this pain: "But at midnight Paul and Silas
were praying and singing hymns to God" (v. 25). This is the singing
spoken about in this present verse from the Paraklesis, a singing that
enters our hearts and sounds forth praises to God despite any circumstances we may face.

Lull the tempest of all my sins, and bestill the raging of passion with thy calm. For progenitress art thou of Him who is Lord and helmsman, O thou Bride of God.

To a great extent, sin rages in confusion, madness, and disorientation. Imagine if God stood continually before us—His beauty and holiness would so dazzle us that we would have no time to sin, no distractions that would make us turn our backs on Him. But even though He is indeed constantly with us, we turn our backs on Him and sin against His will for our lives. How can this be? How can we so often, as they say, "bite the hand that feeds us" so carelessly, unless it were the fault of some madness?

Sin darkens the mind. It convinces us that we can obey Satan's will, and not God's, and it really won't matter. It even questions whether God exists at all. Can you imagine this? It tries to convince us that we can live a balanced life that doesn't lean too much toward either God or the devil. It claims that normal, good people live peaceful and uncommitted lives.

Yet, that uncommitted life is anything but peaceful. The Paraklesis gives us the perfect picture—we are like a tiny ship tossed about in a raging tempest, with no rudder and no means of propulsion. Sometimes the ship points in the right direction, but just as often the wind points us straight toward some danger. What can be more helpless? The *raging of passions* threatens to break the ship apart and destroy us. We shall perish, wrecked and drowned with no hope!

Did the disciples not feel this as they crossed the Sea of Galilee in the storm (Matthew 14:22–33)? How easily storms can develop on the water; one moment you're enjoying a meditative scene, and the next you find yourself wondering what it will be like to die by drowning. When the storm started, and the wind was against them, they thought they had no hope, but hope came to them walking on water and He saved them. Jesus, the gift to the world of His Mother, the *Bride of God*, calmed the storm and made the water stop its raging.

So it is with you. The Savior comes to the helm of your tiny ship and steers the vessel in the right direction. Will the journey go easily? No. Will He make everything go faster? No. Can you forget all about the journey, since Jesus Himself stands at the wheel, and go pay attention to something different? Not at all. But there's something better than all this. There's someone driving who knows the way, and will stay with you and your little craft until you reach a safe harbor. Praise God!

> *O bestow out of the abyss of thy great compassion on me, thy supplicant, for thou didst bring forth One compassionate, who is Savior of all who sing hymns to thee!*

She stood alone (for even though there were some with her, she was most alone in these hours) at the foot of the cross, watching her only child die slowly and painfully. She had always known the inevitability of the task of His sacrifice for the salvation of the world. She had even taught her Son Jesus that this moment would come, when as a child He sensed in His spirit that He had come to the earth for some great purpose. His Mother then urged Him to be strong—but how, now on the awful Golgotha hill, could she herself be strong? How, if not from an abyss—an endless supply—of great compassion?

Let us never forget to whom this great compassion is directed: The Theotokos was strong for you and me. Whereas we live our whole lives in a confused tangle of self-love, the Theotokos, and the compassionate Son she brought forth, bring salvation to the world through their self-sacrifice and giving.

"Behold your mother!" (John 19:27). Behold your mother! She is again sad, weeping for the one who is dying slowly—you! We live in a world where the avoidance of pain has become our first and last priority. We keep our old people alive by machines to avoid the pain of grief. We kill unborn babies so as to avoid the pains of parenthood. We compromise our beliefs to avoid the pain of embarrassment. We give our money to wealthy professionals who help us avoid all kinds of personal pain, and rob the poor. We lounge on padded pews when we go to church, to avoid the pain in our feet. What pain is there that we don't try to avoid? What truth is there that we would not slice apart on the altar of the avoidance of pain?

Behold your mother! Her compassion benefits you, and it calls you to a deeper place than any place you have ever been. The love of the Mother of God benefits us most when we make it our own.

Behold your mother! Look at her face, and recall her ascetic discipline. The disciplines of the Church seem like nothing in comparison to the pain she experienced, and yet our sinful minds and bodies clamor endlessly against them. If the Theotokos had lived with the same selfish mind as is so common in our world, where would we be? Certainly, living in the darkness of sin and death.

Behold your mother, and sing hymns. Allow her holiness to be written on your heart by words of devotion to her.

While delighting, O spotless one, in thy many favors, a hymn of thankfulness do we all raise up in song to thee, knowing thee to be the Mother of our God.

As we sing the Paraklesis we supplicate, but we also give thanks to the Theotokos, whom we know to be *the Mother of our God*. We recognize her delightful and thankful attitude, and in singing to her we desire to make that attitude our own. She has bestowed upon us many favors, even many of which we remain unaware, and will yet bestow many more.

This does not mean that the Mother of God is a good-luck charm that we can carry through our lives as a way of making things go better for us. Some of us carry an icon of the Theotokos in our purse or wallet—a great idea as long as we don't regard her as the equivalent of a lucky rabbit's foot. But then why carry one? This forces us to ask the question: What is our reason for living the Christian life at all?

The danger of the peace and security that our Christian faith brings us is that we may come to see it simply as an easy way to live comfortably and worry-free in this world, and not as a way to serve God above all things. Certainly, some who always carry an image of the Theotokos with them say that the Mother of God helps bring to mind the commandments that we should follow, and others may say that her presence gives them peace. Indeed, how much good comes to us through Mary! How many times do we forget, yet she reminds us! How many times are we in danger, yet her intercessions before the Son rescue us! And still, our *hymns of thankfulness* raised in song to her come from us because we know we raise them to *the Mother of our God*. We thank her for who she is, whatever the circumstances we face.

Sometimes life doesn't turn out the way we would have liked. It often seems that when we come to danger, the danger overwhelms us. In such cases, giving thanks is a great ascetic discipline, as when we might give thanks after a sleepless night or some other trial. We cannot, at these times, rely on our feelings to remind us to give thanks, because we may have no thankful feelings. Feelings are the passions about which the church fathers warn us, and they guide the flesh spoken of by St. Paul. We must respect them, but we cannot trust them. On popular television programs, it may be presented as a good thing to "follow your heart" or "go with your feelings," but if we follow this advice, we die spiritually.

Rather, we must look to the advice of St. Paul, simply put: "In everything give thanks" (1 Thessalonians 5:18).

Having thee as our staff and hope and as our salvation's unshaken battlement, from all manner of adversity are we then redeemed, O thou all-lauded one!

When we regard the Theotokos as the *battlement* of our *salvation*, a protection and help for us, we avail ourselves of a great and steadfast example for our lives. We see in the Theotokos humility, faithfulness, grace, peace, and honor, and we constantly strive to make these qualities our own. We use her as a *staff*, which helps us to stand solidly when we get tired; we look to her in *hope*, and she reminds us of the infinite joy of the age to come; we run to her *unshaken battlement*, because she helps us put into perspective the hundreds of annoying people, undeserved sufferings, hidden costs, sudden illnesses, inconveniences great and small, and rapid passing of the days and years in our lives. We have her as our staff and hope, and as our salvation's unshaken battlement.

But what then? We are *then redeemed* from *all manner of adversity*. What is it to be redeemed from adversity? We know that Christ our Savior redeems us from sin, and that He Himself was the ransom that saved us. But His Mother intercedes for our redemption from adversity. Her attitude toward her own suffering gives the trouble in our lives meaning and grace.

When we use the word "redeemed," on one level we mean "freed." But on another level, we say that something returns to its true nature when it is redeemed. I might have in my home several coupons held to the front of the refrigerator by a magnet. What good are they? No good at all, until I take them to the store and use them to save a little money. The coupon is not "set free" when I redeem it, but in using it I fulfill its meaning. I accomplish the reason of its existence. This is just one of the meanings of the word "redeem" in this verse from the Paraklesis. When we have the Theotokos as our staff, our hope, our battlement, then we gain the peace to understand the true nature of adversity. We come to understand our participation in the suffering of God when we suffer. Our suffering, in her, is redeemed.

Scripture Reading:
Proverbs 31:10–31

Who can find a virtuous wife?

For her worth is far above rubies.

The heart of her husband safely trusts her;

So he will have no lack of gain.

She does him good and not evil

All the days of her life.

She seeks wool and flax,

And willingly works with her hands.

She is like the merchant ships,

She brings her food from afar.

She also rises while it is yet night,

And provides food for her household,

And a portion for her maidservants.

She considers a field and buys it;

From her profits she plants a vineyard.

She girds herself with strength,

And strengthens her arms.

She perceives that her merchandise is good,

And her lamp does not go out by night.

She stretches out her hands to the distaff,

And her hand holds the spindle.

She extends her hand to the poor,

Yes, she reaches out her hands to the needy.

She is not afraid of snow for her household,

For all her household is clothed with scarlet.

She makes tapestry for herself;

Her clothing is fine linen and purple.

Her husband is known in the gates,

When he sits among the elders of the land.

She makes linen garments and sells them,

And supplies sashes for the merchants.

Strength and honor are her clothing;

She shall rejoice in time to come.

She opens her mouth with wisdom,

And on her tongue is the law of kindness.

She watches over the ways of her household,

And does not eat the bread of idleness.

Her children rise up and call her blessed;

Her husband also, and he praises her:

"Many daughters have done well,

But you excel them all."

Charm is deceitful and beauty is passing,

But a woman who fears the LORD, she shall be praised.

Give her of the fruit of her hands,

And let her own works praise her in the gates.

There is nothing that a good woman cannot do. But she does not do all these things for herself, but to serve her husband, her family, and God.

Chapter Six

Ode Five

Lord, enlighten us by Thy precepts and by Thy commands, and by the power of Thy lofty arm bestow Thy peace upon us all, as Thou art the Friend of man.

What does salvation offer us? What benefits await the man who builds a relationship with God in Jesus Christ? Christianity offers Truth, and the *peace* that comes from knowing that we live a life full of truth and light. If we desire anything else from Christianity—such as wealth, comfort, happiness, community respect, and so on—we deceive ourselves as to the meaning of Christ's sacrifice for us. Jesus submitted Himself to the cruel death on the cross so that we might obtain forgiveness of sins, and by our forgiveness we gain peace with God. But the peace that God offers us comes to us by way of our obedience to His *precepts* and His *commands*. Obedience, and the peace that obedience brings, is the end of our search, but not the beginning. Our spiritual healing begins in God's love and grace, and has nothing to do with our effort. The power of God's *lofty arm* is not ours so that we can realize all our earthly desires, lusts, and passions. Salvation is God Himself, who is everything. We dwell in peace when we are obedient to God. We live in the peace that comes from knowing God. It is not knowledge that enlightens us, but obedience to Him. However—

Pure one, fill my heart with rejoicing unto plentitude, and grant thine undefiled felicity, since thou didst give birth unto Him who is the cause of joy.

—having said that, we also *rejoice* to know that the Lord and His Mother do indeed concern themselves with our happiness. They want our hearts to be full of *joy*.

In the first verse of this ode, we remind ourselves about the origin of peace—obedience. And having reminded ourselves of this important truth, we sing the second verse, in which we discover joy in the smile of the Theotokos. Our flesh tells us that obedience is onerous to us: difficult, old-fashioned, worthless, humiliating. And yet, the joy that floods our soul when we learn to obey God tells us something completely different. It tells us that He *is the cause of joy*, and that the Mother of God holds an *undefiled felicity*, a pure joy, which she grants to those who seek it. When we look to her for this joy, we find it, and drink it in until our hearts are filled to overflowing.

We do not obey God in order to take pride in obedience, but we obey and gain the peace with God that obedience brings. Peace with God *fills* our *hearts with rejoicing unto plentitude*.

> *Come deliver us out of dangers, O pure Mother of God, since thou art mother of deliverance, and of the peace which doth surpass all human reasoning.*

There are two kinds of dangers: those you can see and measure with your reason, and those that threaten the spirit, which you often cannot see.

As we sing this verse of the Paraklesis, we pray that the Mother of God may *deliver us out of dangers* and give us peace beyond *human reasoning*. Why beyond reasoning? Because we may not see with the eyes of our reason that we have indeed been delivered from danger. Think of the martyrs, some of whom undoubtedly prayed and asked for deliverance from their tormentors. Were those prayers answered? Yes, by all means, those prayers were answered. God may not have immediately delivered them from their visible enemies, but He did deliver them from the enemy that kills the soul and takes it to everlasting sorrow. These invisible enemies threaten our eternal souls; they endanger us in ways that we detect not with our reason, but with our spirit. From these enemies our Lord delivers all His children, even though our earthly sensibilities may not detect this deliverance.

How often do we find ourselves praying for those things that refer only to this life, to our own desires? And how often do we think we know what things we need deliverance from, and when is the best time? But how silly are these prayers, considering that God holds all things in His hand, and He loves us. First, we need the help that comes from God in order to detect the dangers that threaten our souls. Then we need the grace to begin praying for the most important thing, the *peace which doth surpass all human reasoning.*

> *Dissipate the gloom of my trespasses, O Bride of God, with the clear brightness of thy radiance, for thou didst bear the light divine, which was before all time.*

We started by singing praises to the Birthgiver of the cause of peace, then the cause of joy, and here, the cause of light. This verse illustrates the final step in a lifelong progress toward the acquisition of the Holy Spirit and the vision of the light that is God's greatest grace to His children on earth.

Often in the Holy Scriptures, those who experience a vision of God describe it as something like seeing brilliant light. Moses, Isaiah, Peter, James, and John—all of them saw brilliant light at their closest moments with God. St. Basil the Great called this light the beauty of God, and St. Gregory Palamas made the distinction between the light as the energies of God versus His essence. But no matter who teaches us about the light, the teaching is always the same. What do we learn about God from the fact that those who see Him describe what they see as light?

First, God longs to give His children knowledge. Light is a revealing energy, an informing energy, something we use to discover things, not to hide them.

Second, the knowledge God has to give in Himself does not come to us through study, nor from mysteries that can be shared with some people and not with others (like a secret society); rather, it comes directly from one's commitment to a relationship with God. God makes Himself available to everyone.

And third, God wants us to see Him. I remember when I first heard the Orthodox teaching about the Taboric Light, as the vision of God is sometimes called (after the Mount Tabor of the Transfiguration). I thought it sounded rather odd. See God? Why would I want to see God? I thought that if God wanted me to enter into some higher plane of relationship with Him, I would rather receive some miracle-working power, or clairvoyance, or something like that. Many gifts seemed to be better than to see a brilliant light. But I thought wrong. The reality of the Taboric Light reminds us that God wants us to dwell in Him, and to gaze at Him, to worship Him—not only to go to Him for what we need or want, nor only to use Him as a source of power over the elements of this world, nor only to spend a fixed amount of time with Him each day or week and then be on our way. God wants us to call Him to mind continually in order to worship Him, and know Him, and see Him, *the light divine which was before all time.*

> *Heal me, O pure one, of the sickness that the passions bring. And make me worthy of thy guardianship, and by thy prayers and intercessions grant thou health to me.*

Christians turn to the Church to ask for healing from various bodily diseases and injuries, and priests take time to go to hospitals to pray with the people there. As St. James tells us, we must indeed do these things: "Is anyone among you sick? Let him call for the elders of the church, and let them pray over him, anointing him with oil in the name of the Lord" (James 5:14).

But all people, physical conditions aside, have a greater disease, a greater injury, and a greater need than those things that may be addressed by physicians or hospitals. We have our passions and the *sickness that the passions bring,* which turn us away from the Living God, which turn us toward our own selfishness again and again. A passion is not simply a sin, but a sin that has been repeated so many times that the sin controls the person. The passions are those habits we have that represent the mature flowering of our surrender to sin—the grand limits of our selfishness. They are our spiritual death.

We need healing when we are sick with the passions just as much as we do when a consuming cancer fills our bodies. The cancer may seem like a much more urgent matter, and from one perspective, it is—we might find ourselves praying for healing from cancer in order to live long enough to find healing from the passions. This is why the church fathers have often regarded bodily infirmities as one way God uses to bring us back to Himself: "For this reason many are weak and sick among you, and many sleep. For if we would judge ourselves, we would not be judged. But when we are judged, we are chastened by the Lord, that we may not be condemned with the world" (1 Corinthians 11:30–32).

Did you read that carefully? Your physical suffering comes upon you in order to chasten you, and bring you back to a right relationship with the Lord. So when we ask the Theotokos for healing, we do right to ask for healing from the *sickness that the passions bring.*

Scripture Reading:
Hebrews 2:10–18

For it was fitting for Him, for whom are all things and by whom are all things, in bringing many sons to glory, to make the captain of their salvation perfect through sufferings. For both He who sanctifies and those who are being sanctified are all of one, for which reason He is not ashamed to call them brethren, saying:

"I will declare Your name to My brethren;

In the midst of the assembly I will sing praise to You."

And again:

"I will put My trust in Him."

And again:

"Here am I and the children whom God has given Me."

Inasmuch then as the children have partaken of flesh and blood, He Himself likewise shared in the same, that through death He might destroy him who had the power of death, that is, the devil, and release those who through fear of death were all their lifetime subject to bondage. For indeed He does not give aid to angels, but He does give aid to the seed of Abraham. Therefore, in all things He had to be made like His brethren, that He might be a merciful and faithful High Priest in things pertaining to God, to make propitiation for the sins of the people. For in that He Himself has suffered, being tempted, He is able to aid those who are tempted.

Our Lord's ability to bring us to glory came from His willingness to become like us and suffer in the flesh. And when we become like Him, we also suffer with Him "in things pertaining to God" (v. 17).

Chapter Seven

Ode Six

Entreaty do I pour forth unto the Lord, and to Him do I proclaim all my sorrows, for many woes fill my soul to repletion, and lo, my life unto Hades has now drawn nigh. Like Jonah do I pray to Thee: Raise me up from corruption, O Lord, my God!

Like the last verse of Ode Five, the first verse of Ode Six addresses the subject of the passions.

Each year of my life, in fact, I might say that each time I pray, I learn more about the mystery of repentance. I learn more about the poverty of my soul. I learn more about how so many of my actions during the course of any day are self-serving. Thus I discover that the Christian faith does not exist so that I might feel good about myself, but so that I might come face to face with that loathsome obstacle between myself and God that is my sinfulness.

I want to *pour entreaty to the Lord*, and to *proclaim* to Him *all my sorrows*. But what is the nature of my entreaty? Most of the words I pray, most of the woes I bring to the Lord have only to do with my desire for comfort and honor. Too often, I express a greater longing for material security than for God, a greater love for the things of this world than for serving God. And I am even so ignorant as to express my love for the things of this world to God Himself: "Oh God, make my life comfortable and keep annoying people away from me. Amen." Then, to heap sin upon sin, I blame God and doubt His love when I don't get the things I want. What greater proof do I have of God's abundant love than this, that He has never abandoned me in anger and disgust? My sin is so complex, with twisting layers of selfishness, greed, laziness, and arrogance, that I wonder how God sees any hope for me.

This verse speaks of *corruption*, the corruption that every human shares. We have this corruption in common, and yet we try to hide our corruption from everyone else. We're ashamed of ourselves, or should be, and this shame makes us angry and depressed. *Many woes*, many layers and levels and knots of woes fill my soul to its gluttonous *repletion*, and all I can do is cry out to God for forgiveness: "*Raise me up!* I don't even know how You can raise up a man like me, but I pray that You will."

> *My nature, held by corruption and by death, hath He saved from out of death and corruption, for unto death He Himself hath submitted. Wherefore, O Virgin, do thou intercede with Him who is in truth thy Lord and Son, to redeem me from enemies' wickedness.*

Human beings, when left to their natural inclination, seem to think only of themselves. Even when I do something that seems totally thankless, anonymous, or misunderstood, I do it because I know that I'll feel good afterwards. I'll feel as if I've done the right thing, and I'll mentally pat myself on the back. See how difficult it is to escape from selfishness and pride?

One time I was honored as the manager of a group of people for a project we had completed. One person who spoke referred to me as "selfless." But as I sat and listened to him speak, I thought about how much I thought only of myself when I tried to do my best. I remembered all those times I got into my car at the end of the day and looked at myself in the rearview mirror, smiling the smile of a man who had done a good job, the smile of a successful man. Selfless? Not at all. I was as self-absorbed as anyone could have been, and it made me even more proud that people told me that I had looked rather humble doing it.

How often we deny pride, and thus give in to it. How often we take pride in our ability to act humble!

At baptism we received the tools necessary to provide an escape from this vicious cycle. Sin and pride are very real, but they work from the outside of the baptized Christian. God has redeemed your and my true inner nature. Even though it may sometimes seem as if sin has completely defeated us, it certainly has not. Our nature is no longer a slave to sin, but since we are crucified with Christ we no longer live, but

Christ lives in us (Galatians 2:20). The life we live, we live by His faith.

If you drive across a bridge that has been damaged in some way and has become so out of balance that you feel in danger of sliding off, you don't suddenly change your mind about the nature of bridges. One broken bridge would not lead you to believe that bridges exist only to throw cars into rivers. Rather, you realize that some outside force has altered the bridge so that its original nature has been lost. A storm, time, gravity, poor workmanship, explosives, a large vehicle accident, or something else has introduced damage and danger into the character of that particular bridge. But its nature has not changed—it's still a bridge, built to carry cars across water or a ravine.

So it is with Christians. We have died with Christ and been raised again, but an outside force has damaged us to the extent that our true nature seems to—only *seems* to—have been lost. And so we need repair. The sins that we have committed have harmed us, and have hurt the world around us in mysterious, lasting, and fundamental ways. When I sin, I don't suddenly develop a runny nose, an ear infection, or bad eyesight. My sin touches the very foundation of human life, it hastens another man's death, it spoils history, it contributes imperceptibly to my own separation from God. How can I fight this? How can this be repaired? It is only when God absorbs into Himself the penalty of my sin that I can be forgiven. The outcome of sin must go somewhere, and God has agreed to take it into Himself, so that we might go free: "And you know that He was manifested to take away our sins, and in Him there is no sin" (1 John 3:5).

This verse from the sixth ode of the Paraklesis gives us two perspectives on how we might accept God's forgiveness. First, we ask for the help of His Mother. That is to say, we not only pray to God, but we ask others to pray for us as well. What can be easier? When you turn your attention to God, and just speak, He listens, and His Mother is quick to hear, quicker than any friend you might call. We live in a society built on easy access to information and communication, but still the quickest and most effective communication is prayer.

Secondly, we long to escape from the *wickedness* of our *enemies*. This refers to Satan and his servants, who hold human souls in bondage. We must always remember that sin is bondage. It may seem that a teenager who sneaks out to do something against his parents' wishes, or an adult who wishes ill to a neighbor, or anyone who takes advantage of what is lawful in our society, but clearly not moral—that all these people are only doing what they want to do. But sinning is not what baptized Christians want to do, it's what Satan wants us to do. How often we side with the enemy, rather than with our Savior, who calls us back to the nature He gave us at our spiritual birth!

What are the tools we have been given to fight against the influence of the evil one in our lives? We pray and struggle. Pray to God and the saints, and struggle against sin. In this way, the soul comes to see its true nature revealed, and enjoys God. We are redeemed from the *enemy's wickedness.*

> *I know thee as the protection of my life and most safe fortification, O Virgin! Disperse the horde of my many temptations, and put to silence demonic audacity. Unceasingly I pray to thee, from corruption of passions deliver me!*

Again, the Paraklesis addresses the subject of the passions—thanks to God! We need to carefully and patiently consider this most important issue.

As used by the great spiritual writers of the Orthodox faith, "passion" does not mean "an intense desire for something," a meaning that the word commonly carries in English. Using this meaning, some passion is good: We should have a passion for God, for holiness, for resisting sin, for loving others. In English, the word "passion" can also refer to the suffering of Christ on the cross, as in the "St. Matthew Passion" by J. S. Bach or the 2004 Mel Gibson film, *The Passion of the Christ.* But that is not the meaning we are dealing with here either.

This is an example of a word that doesn't translate well into English. In the writings of the church fathers, "passion" refers to sickness of soul, surrender to sin, the habit of turning your back on God, the darkening of the eye of the soul, demonic audacity, the pollution of the senses. The passions lead us into darkness and away from salvation in Jesus Christ. The passions are the thorns that our Lord told us would cut off the growth of the word of God in our lives (Luke 8:14). When we give ourselves over to bondage to a particular sin, we embrace a passion.

In other words, we all carefully construct the passions that destroy our spiritual lives, like a nation carefully building a great weapon—only to present it to their enemies so that it can be used for evil purposes. Giving in to passion means being tricked into embracing self-destructive behavior. For instance, when God calls us, through the Church, to fast on a particular day, the demons quickly rush to our side to tell us that we should have the freedom and maturity to say no to the fast and to eat whatever we want. "You are not a child," they whisper, "and don't need a priest to tell you what to eat and what not to eat." It is in this way that some excuse themselves from fasting. And yet, these excuses do not express any kind of freedom or spiritual maturity. They simply tell us that whenever the demons tell us to follow them (and not God), our passions throw us down with our foreheads to the floor and make us say, "Yes, master, I will do what you want me to do."

The Theotokos is our *safe fortification* and our *protection*. First, we turn to her because she can help us to see where demonic audacity controls us. How do I know when I'm bowing down to the demons' bidding? The Theotokos *puts to silence* the *demonic audacity* by *delivering* us from the *corruption of passions*; in other words, by pointing to those places where sin has become so habitual that we no longer see it as sin. We cannot continue to feed our passions when we run to the Theotokos for shelter and protection. When we meditate upon the Theotokos, upon her obedience and her godliness, we come to see just how far short we're falling of God's expectations.

The revelation of our sinfulness comprises the first step toward the control and elimination of passions. It's not always comfortable in the shelter of the Theotokos—because it's often there that we become sensitive to our falling-short!

> *A safe retreat art thou to us, and of souls art thou the perfect salvation, and a relief in distresses, O Maiden, and in thy light do we ever exult with joy. O Lady, do thou also now from all passions and dangers deliver us.*

Like the phrase "Most Holy Theotokos, save us," which we examined in the first chapter, the phrase *of souls art thou the perfect salvation* may cause some confusion, a confusion we will again discuss. Does the

Paraklesis express a heretical concept here, that is, salvation in the name of the Theotokos rather than in Christ alone?

Absolutely not. The same principles that the Scriptures express are also expressed by the Church, and the loudspeaker proclaiming them is the blood of those martyrs who died because they would not deny their Lord, Jesus Christ. This present phrase from the canon to the Mother of God, *of souls art thou the perfect salvation*, describes for us two very important aspects of Mary's presence in the Church. Let's look at them separately.

First, when we say, "you are salvation" to the Mother of God, this certainly cannot refer to our eternal salvation, or to the forgiveness of sin. The task of forgiving sin belongs to God alone, through the sacrifice of Jesus Christ, although it may be mediated by others (for instance, in the sacrament of confession). But God alone can be called on for our soul's salvation. "You are salvation," then, must refer to something else—but what?

We love the Theotokos and honor her because our salvation depends not only on the gospel itself, but on the many faithful Christians who carried that gospel to us. The atoning work of Jesus Christ saves us from sin; however, in addition to His atoning work, the Holy Spirit needed to speak to a whole line of Christians down through history who brought the message of salvation to us. We recognize and honor the saints, because without them the world today would have no connection to our Lord's resurrection. Perhaps someone might say that we would still hear about salvation in Christ because God would preserve the message and bring it to all generations, and I agree. But how does God bring the message of salvation to all generations? Through people. People who have given of themselves, perhaps even given their very lives in service to Him and to us. People who have translated and printed the Scriptures and other books. The Theotokos is the first of these people. She is the prototype of evangelists, martyrs, teachers, and intercessors.

What if you made a list of everyone who has significantly influenced your spiritual life—authors, teachers, clergy, family, friends? In her own quiet way, the Theotokos is at the top of the list.

We call her the perfect salvation of our souls because she is perfected in obedience. But likewise, we call Mary the perfect salvation of souls because salvation was perfectly expressed in the Incarnation, and the Incarnation was Mary's work. When she communicated to us the message of salvation, it wasn't through a book, a lecture, an organization, or a work of art. It was given to us by her delivery of God Himself to our world, and by her nurturing of God Incarnate during the years of His youth.

> *Bedridden I lie supine with sickness now, and no healing for my flesh is existent, except for thee who didst bear the world's Savior, our God, the healer of every infirmity. I pray to thee, for thou art good. From corruption of illnesses raise me up!*

For Christians, there is no such thing as luck. Using the word "luck" suggests a particular attitude about the world, an attitude which says that everything happens randomly, and that good things and bad things come to people according to no intelligent influence. We may sometimes feel this is the case in our day-to-day lives, because we often can't explain why things happen the way they do. However, even though Christians can't always explain the reasons for certain events (although some try), we cannot declare that events occur randomly. We understand that God and the devil continually battle over the souls of human beings, and that this world is the battleground. Beyond this, what can we say? I can say that when I look back over the full scope of my life, I see how God has been using every possible means to lead me to Him. Even the bad things, suffering and disappointment, have been a part of that process.

When we realize that this is the case, we can pray that God would give us a spiritual attitude toward suffering. Although we may pray to be healed of a disease, or released from the discomfort of a particular situation, we also understand that God may be calling us to accept suffering as a part of His divine plan. So, we must struggle to give our suffering to Him, as an offering and as a service. This is a very difficult thing to learn, and while we're learning this lesson, we often find ourselves to be very impatient towards God and perhaps even doubtful of His power. This impatience and doubt is the *corruption of illnesses*. From this corruption, from this sin, we need healing—we don't simply need the healing of the physical symptoms of diseases.

Imagine yourself fighting on a medieval battlefield. The situation doesn't look good—you're tired, wounded, thirsty, and surrounded by strong enemy forces. Just as you're about to lose hope, just as you're starting to expect the one stroke that will finish you, your king rides confidently across the battlefield. At one point he looks right at you, and you look right into his eyes. In that glance, you're reminded of a greater purpose, of your home and family, of duty to your country. And you also know for the one moment that the king himself has seen you. He knows what's happening to you. He knows what you're enduring. What impact would this have? There have been times in history when this kind of scenario has decisively influenced a battle.

The king won't throw you a bandage, or take your place for a few minutes while you rest, or jump down off his horse to offer you a drink. But that's not the point. The point is that he knows, he sees, he exists. That's as practical as the help that comes from him gets. But it's enough.

One more point about this particular verse from the Paraklesis. Many times I've sung these words and thought that they cannot refer to me. I'm not *bedridden*, I'm not *supine with sickness*.

But what happens to me when life is so busy that I have no time to pray? Do I get up one hour earlier than normal to make the time? Sadly, I can say that most of the time the answer is no. And what about the nighttime? When I'm so tired I can barely walk up the steps to my bedroom, do I hurry toward the bed or the icons? The bed, I fear. So it's not a complete misstatement to say that I'm confined to my bed, in the same way that one who is addicted to something lives a life controlled by the desire for that thing. I need to pray these words as much as everyone whose physical illness literally confines him to a bed.

Scripture Reading:
Luke 11:27–28
And it happened, as He spoke these things, that a certain woman from the crowd raised her voice and said to Him, "Blessed is the womb that bore You, and the breasts which nursed you!" But He said, "More than that, blessed are those who hear the word of God and keep it!"

Mary had given her Son to the world, for its salvation, for yours and mine, too. His brothers opposed Him, until at least two of them witnessed the resurrection (St. James of Jerusalem and St. Jude). So we know that the Theotokos would not have come to ask our Lord to discontinue His ministry on her own, but we can see how His brothers might. And how would they oppose Him? They would remind Him of His obligation to support His Mother—an obligation He had because she had no other children. If the brothers who came to see Him that day were the children of Mary, why wouldn't they care for her? They didn't want to support her because she was not their mother. Only Jesus was her child. Only Jesus was obligated to support the Theotokos.

When He answered, "My mother and my brothers are these who hear the word of God and do it," this was a message to His brothers: "My obligation now is to the world." Mary knew that. She had prepared her whole life to give up her only Son for the salvation of mankind.

Chapter Eight

The Kontakion to the Theotokos

O protection of Christians that cannot be put to shame, mediation unto the Creator most constant, oh, despise not the suppliant voices of those who have sinned; but be thou quick, O good one, to come unto our aid, who in faith cry unto thee: Hasten to intercession, and speed thou to make supplication, thou who dost ever protect, O Theotokos, them that honor thee.

Many times during the year we sing this Kontakion to the Theotokos, and some might recognize it as the one that is sung, at certain times of the year, as the last of the hymns that come after the Little Entrance in the Divine Liturgy. Orthodox Christians sing it in many languages, translations, and manifestations, but it always says essentially the same thing. In the Paraklesis, this Kontakion appears just before the seventh ode, so we too pause from looking at the verses of the odes to consider it.

Both the first and last lines of this hymn refer to the *protecting* quality of the Theotokos. "Protection" is something that focuses on the future. The Theotokos cannot protect us from something that has already happened, but only from something that has yet to happen. For instance, if I look in the newspaper in the morning and see that the day will start out warm but become cold and rainy later on, I tell my children to take their raincoats to school with them. They complain. They don't want to carry their coats, and they're certainly not going to wear them in the morning when the weather is warm and dry. But I know better, having suffered many times because I didn't prepare properly, and I make them take their coats with them despite their protests. Now, I realize that at some point, they will have to suffer on their own for not having prepared themselves for the weather, and then they'll learn their lesson. But until that time, up until my children have grown enough to make their own decisions about such things, I make it my responsibility to act maturely for them. I protect them.

So it is with our spiritual lives. We grow or shrink, passing from one phase to another. Look at your own life—you have some years of spiritual life behind you, some good and some bad. Your progress has not been steady, just as a fourteen-year-old acts sometimes like a mature adult and sometimes like an infant. And it seems as if long periods of time pass when you're not progressing at all. "Perhaps," you may think, "I've arrived and don't need to grow any more." That attitude is, in itself, one step in the spiritual life. We're always moving and changing, advancing and retreating, learning and forgetting, sprinting and staggering, even when we may see nothing in particular going on.

Your Mother watches over you, as mothers are wont to do. She smiles when you make some gain, and she prays when she sees you fall. As you totter toward some danger, she hurries ahead to remove it, shield you, or warn you in some way, knowing what will come. She is the *protection of Christians*, and when we sing this hymn to her with our hearts thankful for her help, she becomes for us a protection *that cannot be put to shame*, a protection that never fails. She knows how Christians grow in their faith, and she is always one step ahead of us, helping us to move forward.

But how does she accomplish this protection? Through her prayers for us before her Son, our God. She does not protect us by removing every possible sadness from our lives—in this way she differs from the example I gave of myself. No matter what I see that may hurt my children, I try to remove it from their experience—at least when they're little. But we are not infants, and so the Theotokos might by her gaze simply offer us a warning rather than removing the trouble altogether.

It is not God's will that all trials be removed from our lives. When He spoke to St. Peter, predicting the denials that would emerge from the tumultuous events following His arrest, He said, "Simon, Simon! Indeed, Satan has asked for you, that he may sift you as wheat" (Luke 22:31). What an incredible wealth of spiritual insight we may gain from this one sentence! What does it mean that Satan "asked for" St. Peter? If anyone would know about such things, it would be our Lord, and He would also truthfully convey to us the nature of unseen reality. His words clarify the opening of the Book of Job, the part that takes place in heaven, when Satan comes before God and asks permission to harass Job, God's most faithful servant. Does this really happen? Does Satan appear before God and demand permission to badger certain spiritual giants? Our Lord tells us this happens. "Satan has asked for you," He tells St. Peter. In the back of St. Peter's mind, as his Lord stood before Him saying these words, I can imagine a little voice asking, "Did He just say what I thought He just said?"

"That he may sift you as wheat." No matter what this metaphor describes, it doesn't sound good. We know that St. Peter found himself so surrounded by enemies and confusion that he actually denied his Lord not once, but three times. I can relate to this, although I think that Satan has never really concentrated his attention on me because I have nothing like the level of faith that St. Peter had. I remember times when people said things about the Church, or the Scriptures, or our Lord Himself that disparaged my faith in some way, or were just plain wrong, and I remained silent or went along because I didn't want to create a stir.

Once I went to someone's place of business to invite him to church. He had been born Orthodox but no longer practiced his faith at all. His business had obviously prospered very well without God, and I sat in his office rather impressed and feeling a little intimidated. He said to me at one point that he had gone to Sunday school as a child, but "of course while we were supposed to be reading the Bible, all the boys had dirty pictures that we passed around." I smiled and said something like, "Of course. Happens all the time."

No cock crowed when I stepped out of his office, but perhaps it was in hearing the ding of the opening elevator doors that I realized how I had betrayed my Church and my faith. What had I said? I never brought dirty pictures to Sunday school, and none of my friends did either! And yet, I had tried to make it seem as if this successful businessman and I shared the same kind of attitude about the world, the same confidence and successful drive and so on. The wink and the smile, cut from the same cloth, a shared history. Of course, the man never showed up at church. Why would he? He had essentially asked me if the Church had any reality outside the fact of people gathering together, changed in no way by anything divine or supernatural, and I had agreed that it did not. Why would he come to church for nothing other than to help pay my salary?

I had been caught off guard, sifted, and found unequal to the task. Like St. Peter, only after I had left that place did I realize what had happened. Perhaps because I do not have the same level of faith the apostle had, I did not weep for my sin, but I just sat in my car and felt terrible for the opportunity I had missed. My soul was crushed with the grief of loss, the fear of punishment, the disappointment of God, the debilitating weight of pride and arrogance, and the shame of stupidity.

This is how Satan sifts us as wheat. The test is not on any schedule, and we can't join a study group in order to prepare. We may find ourselves "blind-sided" many times by the same attack before we learn to see it coming. And it is extremely painful every time.

Now, what we really wish Jesus had said to St. Peter is this: "Satan has asked to sift you as wheat, but I won't let him." But he doesn't say that, does He? Jesus tells St. Peter that he will soon suffer a satanic attack, but comforts him only in that He says He will pray for him: "Simon, Simon! Indeed, Satan has asked for you, that he may sift you as wheat. But I have prayed for you, that your faith should not fail" (Luke 22:31–32). This is the same way in which the Theotokos is our protection. She does not remove all obstacles from our way, because that would stifle our spiritual growth, but she lifts us continually before the throne of God that we might receive the strength and grace to persevere, and learn, and develop into mature Christians.

When we were babies in the faith, the Theotokos protected us in the way a mother might protect a baby, but as we grow she becomes our protection in a different way. I may make my children wear their raincoats when they're little, no matter how much they complain about it, but if my teenage children argue with me forcefully enough, I say to them, "Go ahead and go without one. You'll eventually learn." I cannot act as protector to my children in the same way at all levels of their maturity. Ideally, my own maturity allows me to make those kinds of adjustments, just as the Theotokos uses her knowledge of the world and of the spiritual lives of men to fulfill her role as our mother and guide.

And as we mature, we become older siblings, the ones who help the younger children in the faith to prepare themselves for the obstacles

Satan puts in our way, the ways in which he sifts us as wheat. The Theotokos is our mother and protector, but we learn as we grow, and we can then teach others as they make their way through the spiritual life. "And when you have returned to Me, strengthen your brethren" (Luke 22:32b), our Lord said to St. Peter. When you have fallen, pick yourself up and try to teach others not to fall in the same way. Each of us has known someone who exudes a certain spiritual maturity, who provides for us a mature image of the Christian life. We are encouraged and challenged when we are in the presence of that person. His face, or the sound of her voice, the words gently spoken and the way that person sees the world all blend into an image of something we ourselves hope to become. Those are the older siblings, and thanks be to God that we have them.

And who is that person's older sibling? Who is the head among the children in our family? The Theotokos is indeed our mother and guide, but she is also the oldest of our sisters, the first to receive Christ into herself.

Scripture Reading:
Luke 22:31–34

And the Lord said, "Simon, Simon! Indeed, Satan has asked for you, that he may sift you as wheat. But I have prayed for you, that your faith should not fail; and when you have returned to Me, strengthen your brethren." But he said to Him, "Lord, I am ready to go with You, both to prison and to death." Then He said, "I tell you, Peter, the rooster shall not crow this day before you will deny three times that you know Me."

Before trials start, our confidence knows no bounds, as with St. Peter in this passage. Our Lord does not tell him what trials await, but how he will respond to them: "You will deny me."

Here we learn that the particular sufferings we endure do not matter as much as how we respond to them.

Chapter Nine

Ode Seven

Once from out of Judea did the children go down to the land of Babylon. The fire of the furnace they trampled down, while chanting by their faith in the Trinity: O God of our Fathers, blessed art Thou.

This verse refers to a story from the Old Testament, in the Book of Daniel. Daniel has many great and spiritually rewarding stories—every Christian should be familiar with it. The story of the *children* in the *fire of the furnace* begins when the king of Babylon tells everyone that they must worship a golden statue of himself as a god, and three of Daniel's friends refuse. When the king finds out that they will not bow down to the statue, he has them brought before him for questioning. He reminds them that "if you do not worship, you shall be cast immediately into the midst of a burning fiery furnace. And who is the god who will deliver you from my hands?" (Daniel 3:15). The three tell the king that they still refuse to worship his image, and the king commands that they be thrown into the furnace. The king's servants stoke the flames so high that the soldiers who are assigned the task of throwing the Hebrews into the furnace are themselves killed by the fire.

But the king notices something. Even though he only consigned three people to the fire, he can see four of them walking around in the flames, as if strolling through a garden. He then shouts to the three to come out of the fire, and they step out completely unharmed—the Scripture gives us the marvelous detail that their clothes did not even smell like smoke. In awe of this great miracle, the king changes his decree so that it says that no one can speak anything against the God of the Hebrews without suffering severe punishment.

What does this have to do with us? Much. The image of the three Hebrews being thrown into the furnace for refusing to worship false gods is just as critical for us today as it was for those in Daniel's time. A decree has gone up in our time as well, but it's not written anywhere that you can go and see it. This decree has been filtered to us through education, entertainment, social interaction, and in a hundred other ways. It tells us that our comfort is the most important thing we can possess.

Someone I spoke with recently reminded me of this when she said, "At least I have my health, and that is the most important thing." She said it, and I heard it, as an incontestable truth. "Of course," I said automatically, "health is the most important thing." But is it? When I'm praying late at night, a little voice keeps saying, "Go to bed. If you don't go to bed, you'll be tired tomorrow, and then you'll get sick, and that's not what God wants." Which is more important, my health or my relationship with God? Which is more important, sleep or prayer? How can I miss one day of prayer, and still allow a TV to be in my home? Which is more important?

Sometimes I think that there is not just one, but many golden statues that call me away from the worship of the One True God. This is the same God who saved the three Hebrews from the fiery furnace—I want to trust Him that He will take care of me, He will walk with me, the fourth person in the furnace, if I stand up to the false gods of today with the same resolve that those three Hebrews had.

Having willed thus, O Savior, to dispense our salvation in Thine economy, Thou dwelt within the Maiden's womb and unto all creation as protectress Thou showed her forth. O God of our fathers, blessed art Thou.

Some people call themselves Christians, and yet do not honor the Theotokos. Others call themselves Christians, and yet seem to honor *only* the Theotokos, neglecting Christ. Both of these ways provide people with easy answers to spiritual questions—they only have one deity to "worry about." And yet, the reality of the Christian life is very different from either of these two options, because our salvation was accomplished in the cooperation of Christ and His Mother.

The arrangement originated in the mind of God, as it does for every man. Mary, by herself, could not have contrived it so that her Creator and God would dwell in her womb. God *willed thus*. With those who do not honor the Theotokos, we agree on this point. However, after God chose Mary, the cooperation between them started. When the angel delivered God's invitation to Mary to become the Mother of the Incarnate God, the weight of decision fell on her. He asked her permission, and both God and the archangel stood waiting while Mary considered the proposal, while she asked the one question that helped her clarify in her mind what was happening to her.

Ultimately, of course, she agreed to become the God-bearer, the protectress, even of the infant God Himself. The lack of Mary's consent would have thwarted the very dispensation and plans of God. God needed her consent in order to accomplish His plan of salvation for the world, and she gave it. For that one fact, should we not be eternally grateful to her?

But not only to her. Certainly, the Theotokos is the first among the saints, but we also see in the example of her life the extent to which the work and will of God relies upon the agreement of men. There are things right now that God wants to do in the world, people around you that He wants to touch, and you are the instrument by which he wants to accomplish His goals. He cannot act without your cooperation. Even in your own salvation, God needs your unguarded response of trust (the same as that of Mary) before He can give you the gifts He has prepared for you. This is the *dispensation* of the divine *economy*, namely, that our salvation depends on our day-to-day response to God's offering of grace. Listen to the level of cooperation with God to which St. Paul calls the Philippian church: "Therefore, my beloved, as you have always obeyed, not as in my presence only, but now much more in my absence, work out your own salvation with fear and trembling; for it is God who works in you both to will and to do for His good pleasure" (Philippians 2:12–13).

As you have obeyed in the past, so obey now, and even more. As you have embraced the mind of Christ in the past, now embrace it daily, moment by moment. When the divine messenger comes to you with the offering of grace, respond as the Theotokos did, and become the carrier and even protector of Christ, so that you can bring Him to others.

Make request, O pure Mother, to thy Son, who hath willed to grant mercy unto us, to rescue from transgressions and from the soul's defilement those who cry out most faithfully: O God of our fathers, blessed art Thou.

We have already addressed the importance of the intercessions of the Theotokos for us. Indeed, she is praying for you right now—but what is she praying for? Simply that you would be saved? Yes, but more specifically, that you would be saved from sin: from *transgressions*, and from the *soul's defilement*.

But what does this mean for us? It means that salvation does not come without a struggle, particularly a struggle against sin. St. Paul echoes the words of St. Matthew (1:21) when he says to his disciple Timothy, "Christ Jesus came into the world to save sinners" (1 Timothy 1:15) and when he says "[God] has saved us and called us with a holy calling" (2 Timothy 1:9). This is not to say that we make ourselves worthy of salvation, but that we cooperate with God in the work of salvation that He accomplishes in us: "I will show you my faith by my works" (James 2:18).

God has called each of us for a purpose, and nothing stands in the way of His purpose except us ourselves, and the sins to which we continually cling. Because each of us is absolutely unique, God cannot call anyone else to do the work that He has in mind for you—only you know the people you do, say the things you do, live where you live, and so on. The same applies to me. God needs each of us to continue the work He started in Jesus Christ: "Let a man so consider us, as servants of Christ and stewards of the mysteries of God" (1 Corinthians 4:1). Indeed, every Orthodox Christian alive in the world right now guides the Church in his own capacity, because God has made us the stewards of His mysteries.

But what kind of stewards are we? St. Paul continues, "It is required in stewards that one be found faithful" (1 Corinthians 4:2). Every convert who approaches the Church for baptism and chrismation, as well as every family that brings a child for churching and baptism, needs to remember the awesome responsibility of this act. The presence of each Christian in the Church (and all baptized Christians are present in the Church, even if they never attend services) either makes it better or makes it worse, but the Church cannot remain the same.

We receive the gift of salvation, but when we open the gift, we discover that it is a tool. The gift is meaningless unless the tool is used. And for what task did God design this tool? God gives us this gift, this tool, in order to help us struggle against sin: "knowing this, that our old man was crucified with Him, that the body of sin might be done away with, that we should no longer be slaves of sin" (Romans 6:6).

If the Theotokos appeared before you right now, she would tell you to stop sinning. When we pray the Paraklesis to her, we ask her to help us do exactly that.

> *A fount of incorruption and a tower of safety is she who gave Thee birth. A treasure of salvation and portal of repentance hast Thou proved her to them that shout, O God of our fathers, blessed art Thou.*

We address this verse to our Lord. This happens in a number of verses from the Paraklesis, especially the first verse of each ode. Sometimes the words are simply a prayer to Jesus, and other times, as in the present verse, we sing to Him our attitude toward His Mother.

In other verses, the person to whom we sing changes, as with the verse before this one, which speaks at first to the Theotokos (*Make request, O pure Mother . . .*), but ends by addressing God (*O God of our fathers, blessed art Thou*).

So in the Paraklesis, we switch freely back and forth between words addressed to the Lord Jesus Christ and words addressed to His Mother. Often, when the hymn's audience is God Himself, the words describe the Theotokos, as in this verse: *a tower of safety is she who gave Thee birth*. The opposite also occurs, as with the second verse of the sixth ode: *My nature held by corruption and by death hath He saved from out of death and corruption. . . . Wherefore, O Virgin, do thou intercede with Him . . . to redeem me from enemies' wickedness*. We tell the Theotokos about her Son, almost as if to remind her of how much He loves us and has done for us, and then plead with her to intercede with Him on our behalf.

I can remember times when I stood in our church praying the Paraklesis by myself, and turned back and forth from the icon of the

Theotokos to the icon of Christ, depending on to whom each line was addressed. I was trying to be precise in my praying, as I often like to do, but the turning back and forth became a bit much. I stopped it after trying it once or twice. Does it matter to whom you address your prayers? Perhaps you've heard the story about the woman who went into a seemingly empty church to pray. As she knelt, a man painting icons behind the altar thought he might play a trick on her, and started to quietly say things like, "I hear your prayers, I'm listening," and so on. Finally the woman lifted up her head, looked at the icon of Christ, and said, "Jesus, please be quiet. I'm trying to talk with your Mother."

The key, I think, is the relationship you build with someone over the years. Our Lord, His Mother, a particular saint or saints—when you pray to and bless and commemorate them over and over again for a long time, you start to develop a real and loving relationship with a living person. The Theotokos is not God, she cannot be in all places at all times. But she can become for us a *fount of incorruption*, a *tower of safety*, a *treasure of salvation*, and a *portal of repentance* when we continually cry out to her and gain her attention by our prayers and devotion.

> *Deign to grant restoration from diseases of body and soul to those who run to thy divine protection with faith, O Theotokos, and thus grant them recovery. O Mother of Christ our Savior art thou.*

Someone gave me an old Orthodox prayer book, and for a short time I took it to the hospital with me when I went to see people there. But only for a short time. I soon discovered that most of the prayers for the sick were a little tough to swallow, at least for most of those I went to visit. Some people have a level of spiritual maturity that allows them to hear a prayer that says, "Use your sickness to save your soul," as almost all the prayers in this book did. Most people do not. Most want the priest to come to the hospital and pray only that they might get better and go home.

But here, as in so many other parts of the Paraklesis, we link together *diseases of body and soul*. One person might say, "Why me?" or, "I don't deserve this," when sickness or injury upsets his life, but the follower of Christ who understands spiritual things knows that every man is guilty of every sin, and every one of us deserves nothing more or less than death and hell. When I keep this in mind, I'm able to look beyond the pain of my infirmities to the spiritual truths they hold, and thank God, as St. Paul says, always: "giving thanks always for all things to God the Father in the name of our Lord Jesus Christ" (Ephesians 5:20).

Scripture Reading:
Ezekiel 43:27—44:14

"'When these days are over it shall be, on the eighth day and thereafter, that the priests shall offer your burnt offerings and your peace offerings on the altar; and I will accept you,' says the Lord GOD."

Then He brought me back to the outer gate of the sanctuary which faces toward the east, but it was shut. And the LORD said to me, "This gate shall be shut; it shall not be opened, and no man shall enter by it, because the LORD God of Israel has entered by it; therefore it shall be shut. As for the prince, because he is the prince, he may sit in it to eat bread before the Lord; he shall enter by way of the vestibule of the gateway, and go out the same way."

Also He brought me by way of the north gate to the front of the temple; so I looked, and behold, the glory of the LORD filled the house of the LORD; and I fell on my face. And the LORD said to me, "Son of man, mark well, see with your eyes and hear with your ears, all that I say to you concerning all the ordinances of the house of the LORD and all its laws. Mark well who may enter the house and all who go out from the sanctuary. Now say to the rebellious, to the house of Israel, 'Thus says the Lord GOD: "O house of Israel, let us have no more of all your abominations. When you brought in foreigners, uncircumcised in heart and uncircumcised in flesh, to be in My sanctuary to defile it—My house—and when you offered My food, the fat and the blood, then they broke My covenant because of all your abominations. And you have not kept charge of My holy things, but you have set others to keep charge of My sanctuary for you."

"'Thus says the Lord GOD: "No foreigner, uncircumcised in heart or uncircumcised in flesh, shall enter My sanctuary, including any foreigner who is among the children of Israel. And the Levites who went far from me, when Israel went astray, who strayed away from Me after their idols, they shall bear their iniquity. Yet they shall be ministers in My sanctuary, as gatekeepers of the house and ministers of the house; they shall slay the burnt offering and the sacrifice for the people, and they shall stand before them to minister to them. Because they ministered to them before their idols and caused the house of Israel to fall into iniquity, therefore I have raised My hand in an oath against them," says the Lord GOD, "that they shall bear their iniquity. And they shall not come near Me to minister to Me as priest, nor come near any of My holy things, nor into the Most Holy Place; but they shall bear their shame and their abominations which they have committed. Nevertheless I will make them keep charge of the temple, for all its work, and for all that has to be done in it."

See how sacred the holy places were to the ancient Israelites. Shouldn't we also preserve our holy spaces, our churches, altars, and ourselves, with at least the same level of respect?

Chapter Ten

Ode Eight

The King of heaven, whom all the hosts of angels hymn with their chants and praises of glory, praise ye and exalt Him to the ages forever.

Angels continually surround us, and yet we don't see them. Look around you now, do you see any angels? No, and yet at your baptism the priest prayed that God would "yoke unto his life a radiant angel, who shall deliver him from every snare of the adversary, from encounter with evil, from the demon of the noonday, and from evil visions,"[1] and God answered that prayer. The angel assigned to you that day stands near you now.

At each Vespers and Divine Liturgy, and at other services of the Church, the priest refreshes this request for your benefit and the benefit of all the other baptized faithful: "An angel of peace, a faithful guide, a guardian of our souls and bodies, let us ask of the Lord." And before he prays this prayer in the Divine Liturgy, as the priest makes the Little Entrance with the book of the Gospels, he prays to God that angels would accompany the procession: ". . . that with our entrance there may be an entrance of holy angels serving with us and glorifying Thy goodness." At the prayers of the hours, we again make the request of God that He would "encompass us with Thy holy angels, that guided

---

1 *The Service Book of the Holy Eastern Orthodox Catholic and Apostolic Church* according to the use of the Antiochian Orthodox Christian Archdiocese of North America (Englewood, New Jersey, 1971), p. 148.

and guarded by them, we may attain to the unity of the faith and to the knowledge of Thine unapproachable glory"; and again, our Lord honors this request.

How differently we would act if we kept in our minds the presence of this angel of God! In fact, certain prayer books include an evening prayer to our angel for forgiveness for any way in which we have offended him during the course of that day. What a marvelous way of reminding ourselves that a powerful and protecting being watches every step we take and word we speak! When our children were very young, my wife and I hung in their room an old picture of an angel guarding two children as they cross a broken bridge over a raging stream. The picture itself was rather sappy and old-fashioned, but it communicated the reality of the guardian angel, something upon which every parent depends.

But angels do not only protect men, they worship God. And they invite us to join them, as does this verse from the Paraklesis when it says, *praise ye and exalt Him to the ages forever.* Indeed. Listen for their voices, thank God for their protection, and join in their worship.

> *Do not disdain those who seek the aid that thou dost grant, for, O Virgin Maiden, they do hymn thee, and they all exalt thee unto ages forever.*

Notice how this verse relates to the one before it. In the first verse, we recall the angels singing their praises to God, and in the second verse we remind the Theotokos that we ourselves sing her praises. We have become the angels, we have joined them in their song.

Do not disdain us, we sing to Mary. Would she disdain us? Think of the expression a person has when he disdains something—can you imagine this expression on the face of the Mother of God? Certainly not. And yet we pray in the Paraklesis, *Do not disdain those who seek the aid that thou dost grant.* Why pray to avoid something which seems so unlikely? It's like praying every day that I might avoid having a piano drop on my head.

We make this request precisely because we have become the angels singing continually to the glory of God and His Mother. We agree that the Theotokos might overlook our request if we had nothing but a casual relationship with her, because the ones who give her very little of their lives must expect little in return. But when we join the angels exalting her *unto ages forever*, we seek her aid continually. We expect much. We expect that the very Mother of God would hear our songs and smile upon our petitions.

If I meet a famous person and ask for an autograph, and I hand that person a program of some kind and even a pen with the cap off, what do I expect? Only that this person might scribble his name and hand pen and program back to me. But what if that person is my spouse, or my child, or close friend? I don't ask for such casual requests as an autograph, but I ask for more important things, more difficult things, things that express the depth of our relationship. "I'm taking your car. Give me the keys." Or, "I need you to stop at the store." Or, "I'm at the hospital, come right away."

When we pray the Paraklesis, we enter into more than just a casual relationship with the Theotokos. We become part of the family, part of the choir of angels in heaven, continually crying out our love. "Do not disdain us," we pray. "Do not treat us like ones who have no great relationship with you." We pray to the Mother of God, "Treat us like members of your family."

> *On all who hymn thee with faith, O Virgin, and exalt thy truly ineffable Offspring, thou hast poured forth a great abundance of thy cures and healings.*

The famous heretic Nestorius refused to call Mary the "Theotokos"— of all the things he did as the patriarch of Constantinople, this is what we remember him for. Orthodox Christians today might find it hard to understand how he could say such a thing. But when we really try to discern his reasons for his opposition to the term, "Mother of God," we find that Nestorius was trying to make sense out of the Incarnation. His error is the same as that of every heretic from Arius to the Jehovah's Witnesses. They try to make the Incarnation reasonable, and cannot. Anyone who tries to fit the Truth of God into a form comprehensible to men's minds must bend it, maim it, and ultimately destroy it. We cannot shrink the truth to fit our ignorance, and anyone who tries to apply rigorous logic to the gospel of Christ ends up with nothing. "We preach

Christ crucified, to the Jews a stumbling block and to the Greeks fool-ishness" (1 Corinthians 1:23).

In the course of these meditations on the text of the Paraklesis, we've spent time considering the great mystery of the Theotokos. We are not the first generation to do this. Many have looked at her icon and asked themselves: How was God born of her? Our Lord, perfect God and perfect Man? Two natures in one person, neither mixing nor exist-ing separate from one another? These are vast and deep mysteries.

So how can we pray our prayers to the Theotokos and to her Son? We certainly cannot pray unless we believe, and we must know some-thing of the mysteries of God before we can believe. But we will never completely understand these mysteries. We embrace them, accept them, submit to them, and in them find a reason to pray and the will to pray. We hymn the Theotokos *with faith*, and admit the ineffability of her *offspring*.

When I was a Protestant pastor, I went often for personal retreats to a Trappist monastery. Today when I look back I can see that my ques-tioning of my denomination's theology had begun, although I was re-ally unaware of it at the time. At the time I thought I went only for the solitude, the library, the chanting of the hours, and the wonderful grounds of that place.

On the walkway in front of the retreat center stood a huge statue of Mary. One day I stopped to look at the statue, and noticed that the artist had depicted her standing on a snake. "What Mary legend have we here?" I scoffed. As I stood there looking, the retreat master came out of the building and approached me. He introduced himself and we started to talk together. Finally, I asked him about the snake. "In Gen-esis, the Scriptures tell us that the offspring of Adam and Eve will bruise the head of the serpent, the devil," he said. That sounded reasonable— I knew the passage. After we finished our conversation, I went to my room and looked up the passage from Genesis in my Hebrew Bible. At that time, whenever I read from the Old Testament, I read directly from the Hebrew. The passage—Genesis 3:15—did indeed say that the off-spring of the woman would bruise the serpent's head, and the serpent would bruise the offspring's heel, but one thing caught my attention. The passage clearly used the male gender to speak of the offspring— wouldn't that refer to Christ, and not to Mary?

"Aha," I thought, "I've got him." I went back downstairs, and found the retreat master sweeping the front hallway. I confronted him with my brilliant biblical discovery—which really was not so brilliant, since the passage could in fact refer to either male or female offspring, even though the words were masculine. But I had something with which to start an argument, and that's what I wanted. He listened intently to what I said, then smiled, shrugged his shoulders, and continued sweeping. He said nothing. I stood there for a few moments, and then went back to my room, disappointed.

How I had wanted to argue! How I had wanted to show him the errors of the veneration of Mary! Or, perhaps deeper inside my mind, I wanted him to show me the errors of my own way of thinking. Couldn't we fight just a little bit, like good Christian brothers?

His shrug stayed with me all day. At first I thought it said, "Oh, you're too smart for me, I quit." Then later on, I remembered the expression on his face—serene, peaceful, happy. Perhaps, then, I thought, his shrug meant, "Whatever you say, chief. I don't want to talk about it." But the more I remembered each tiny moment of our exchange, the more I came to believe that his silence had really said to me, "This is what my church teaches. You wouldn't understand."

After dinner that night, I asked him. This time, he answered with words. I can't remember them exactly, but essentially he said, "Christ is the offspring of Mary, and St. Luke reminds us, of Adam and Eve. Mary crushed the serpent's head when she gave her Son to the world."

For the second time that day, I said "aha" to myself. This man had something that I wanted—faith. He believed not because he had proven everything for himself, but because he accepted the teachings of his church. He accepted tradition, and I did not. Or at least I thought I didn't. Of course, I didn't realize that the Bible was part of the Tradition I supposedly rejected. I had accepted the authority of the Scriptures the same way this man had accepted Christianity—on faith. Having decided the Scriptures were the unerring word of God, I then set about to create my own Christianity, which I assumed would emerge from my attitude of constant questioning. I thought I had to mistrust everything in order to be an authentic Christian. This monk, the retreat master, did not. He spent his time working out his salvation with fear and trembling, while I spent my time reinventing Christianity.

I had become like the heretics, who spend their time inventing a logical Christian faith. As we meditate upon the reality of the Mother of God, we find that we cannot "wrap our minds" around her mystery, but we nevertheless embrace it, and use the truth of her birthgiving to draw us closer to God.

All the diseases that plague my soul dost thou make well, and the sufferings of the flesh thou healest, wherefore, O thou Maiden full of grace, I glorify thee.

To "glorify" means to shed light upon something, to draw attention to something or someone. When we glorify God, we turn our attention to Him and desire that others would do the same. The glory of God is His brightness, the characteristic that makes us look at Him, think about Him, and worship Him.

We likewise glorify the Theotokos—and why? Because she makes well the *diseases* of our souls, and she also heals the *sufferings of the flesh*. In other words, she works. We don't simply adore the Mother of God because it's a tradition of the Church, but because we have each discovered for ourselves that she is real, and alive, and powerful. The healing that we desire happens when we turn to her.

Sometimes those who have rejected the Church say they believe that the Church has fooled people into believing its claims. I agree that that could be the case for a time, perhaps even for generations. But for two thousand years? What hoax could survive so long? Are there other things that have survived that long and have then—in our enlightened generation—emerged as hoaxes? Love, music, eating, or sleeping? Government or commerce? And what errors can we identify from history that have fallen by the wayside among men: bloodletting and leeches, human sacrifice, ignorance of hygiene, communism, the flat earth? My point is that the things that work survive. The things that don't fall away from popular attention and become the property of academics and outcasts.

I sometimes say to people, "Give God a try." He has a money-back guarantee. When you test Him to see if He is alive, and loving, and effective, you'll discover why so many have followed Him throughout history, why many follow Him today, and why many yet unborn will give their whole lives to Him. And the same holds true for His Mother as well.

All the assaultings of the temptations dost thou quell, and the on-slaughts of the passions banish, wherefore do we hymn thee to all ages, O Virgin.

When I was a child, I loved to watch a TV program called "Captain Kangaroo." Some years later, I played every day with a toy soldier called "G. I. Joe." When I got older, I got my first job, and making money occupied all my attention. Then I started getting serious about music, and that filled my days and nights. If you had asked me at any one of those periods in my life whether my current interest would last forever, I would have vigorously asserted that it would. As a four- or five-year-old, I believed that I would want to watch Captain Kangaroo every day for the rest of my life. But when I started to play with G. I. Joe, the Captain seemed a little too tame. He was for little kids. And then when I started to make my own money, watch out! Where is G. I. Joe? On the floor in my closet!

As we get older, we find that interests come and go. Some people change occupations in the middle of their lives, and some even itch to find new spouses and start second families. But the Church is different from this. We don't change things in the Church just because we're a "new generation," or live in a new century, or whatever. The church is an anchor—the liturgy at which we worship God as children is the same liturgy at which we worship Him as adults. To understand this takes some maturity, it takes time. I sometimes hear young people ask if we can change something in the Church to make it more interesting or up-to-date. Female priests, upbeat music, shorter services, and so on—these suggestions come back again and again when you listen for them. Those who ask for such changes bristle when the Church says no. Some sulk and plot. But haven't other churches already tried to change in order to please the fickle elements of human nature? Haven't they already discovered that change has destroyed their churches and their souls?

This present verse from the Paraklesis reminds us of a very important point. For how long will the interest of the Church in the Theotokos continue? *To all ages.* And how long will your interest in the Mother of God last? Again, *to all ages*; that is, forever.

Scripture Reading:
Proverbs 9:1–12
Wisdom has built her house,

She has hewn out her seven pillars;

She has slaughtered her meat,

She has mixed her wine,

She has also furnished her table.

She has sent out her maidens,

She cries out from the highest places of the city,

"Whoever is simple, let him turn in here!"

As for him who lacks understanding, she says to him,

"Come, eat of my bread

And drink of the wine I have mixed.

Forsake foolishness and live,

And go in the way of understanding.

"He who corrects a scoffer gets shame for himself,

And he who rebukes a wicked man only harms himself.

Do not correct a scoffer, lest he hate you;

Rebuke a wise man, and he will love you.

Give instruction to a wise man, and he will be still wiser;

Teach a just man, and he will increase in learning.

"The fear of the LORD is the beginning of wisdom,

And the knowledge of the Holy One is understanding.

For by me your days will be multiplied,

And years of life will be added to you.

If you are wise, you are wise for yourself,

And if you scoff, you will bear it alone."

Wisdom begins with the fear of the Lord and progresses in correction and rebuke. The humble attitude of the Theotokos gives us a perfect model for the attitude we need to be wise people.

Chapter Eleven

Ode Nine

Most rightly we confess thee as our God's Birthgiver, we who through thee have been saved, O thou Virgin most pure. With choirs of bodiless angels, thee do we magnify.

It is right for us to *confess* the supreme value of the Theotokos. The world longs to hear the truth about unseen realities, the traditional and ancient beliefs of those who have lived before us, and the Mother of our Savior. *Most rightly* do *we confess* to the world our love for the Theotokos.

For a number of years, I started and ended every day by praying the prayers from a little book called *A Pocket Prayer Book for Orthodox Christians*. I don't use it anymore—I have a different prayer routine—but that little book gave me a solid foundation in the faith with the basic prayers of Orthodoxy. I still have my old copy, worn and masking-taped, faded and wrinkled from having gotten wet several times.

In both the morning and evening prayers, my little book asked me to recite the Creed. When I first started using the book, I wouldn't do it. I wanted to pray to God, and to whom is the creed addressed? To the world? To myself? I didn't want to spend time with the technicalities of the faith, with theology and the like. I wanted to pray.

But over time, I started to obey the book's instruction, and included the Creed as part of my morning and evening prayers. I had come to acknowledge a basic spiritual law: What one believes determines how he prays. Obviously, not everyone in the world prays the same way, but what makes their prayers different if not their beliefs? If you believe God is your buddy, or that He only exists to make your life miserable, or that He consists exclusively of the Holy Spirit (or whatever other error you might embrace), this influences how you pray. If you believe in another religion besides Christianity, this also influences your prayers. But if you adhere to the ancient Christian faith, the faith as delivered by our Lord to His disciples, and from them to us, then the words you say when you lift your voice to God reflect that belief. The essentials of this faith are expressed in the Creed, and so we say it often in the context of prayer in order to shape and illuminate the words we say and our sighs.

The whole world needs this truth. Are you willing to proclaim it? Would you confess the Theotokos as the Birthgiver of God? The root of the word "confess" in the Greek language also gave us the word "martyr." Is it a kind of martyrdom to confess to the world the supreme value of the Theotokos, how through her we have been saved? In a way, yes.

As a Protestant, I had a very poor attitude toward the Theotokos, and this attitude gave me a great deal of trouble as I considered converting to Orthodoxy. I was very uncomfortable with the Church's belief about Mary. I had at that time a very good Roman Catholic friend, and I asked him to talk to me about his church's teaching about Mary. He scoffed. "Don't worry about Mary. Mary's for the old women and the kinds of people that see her face in vegetables and on the sides of buildings." His words, of course, offered me no comfort. Did his attitude also reflect popular belief in the Orthodox Church? And if it did, why would I join any church where no one actually believed what the church taught?

Thanks to God, I was able to find an Orthodox priest who sat with me for some hours and listened to my complaints about the Church's theology of the Theotokos. At first, I listened to his defense of Mary thinking, "He has to say this, he's a priest." But after some time, I began to see that he really did believe in the Church's teaching on the subject—and this caused me to look at him with pity. I kept thinking how gullible he must be to admit to these odd and murky teachings (this was my attitude at the time). I almost hated to prove him wrong—everyone feels sorry for simple and naïve people. And truth be told, I thought I was casting pearls before swine when I attempted to discuss theology with anyone like that; after all, I thought, they never listen to reason. But why not? I decided to keep talking with him.

Then I came to a third stage of understanding, as I felt in my heart that what he was saying was correct. I stopped thinking about defending the theology I had held my whole life and started to look at the face of the Theotokos. The Christ within my heart (such as it was) gazed at His Mother, Mary, worthy of praise. I felt the ice melting, and knew that I could make the Orthodox Church my spiritual home.

My attitude toward this Orthodox priest (now a friend and colleague) at the beginning of our conversation has haunted me ever since. Do I really want people to look at me the same way I looked at him? Do I want people to inwardly, or perhaps outwardly, roll their eyes when they hear me *confess* Mary as *God's Birthgiver*?

Yes, I do! The world needs to hear the truth, and yet many fear the truth. The history of the martyrs reminds us of how the world often responds to the revelation of unseen realities. Should we not be happy to join them, the martyrs? Should we not be thankful that all the Lord asks of us is some social discomfort, when they suffered torments and death?

> *The torrents of my weeping, turn not with refusal, for thou didst give birth to Him who doth take away all tears from every face, O thou Virgin, for He is Christ indeed.*

If we could ask the Theotokos why she gave birth to the Savior of the world, she would tell us that she gave Him to us because she knew that mankind labored in sin and despair, and that her Son could set us free. In the explanation offered by the angel, the Theotokos detected and understood the great need of men and how it would happen that her Son would meet that need. He would bring light to those in darkness (Luke 2:32, the song of St. Simeon), but how would He accomplish this? She knew. She would not bring forth a political or military leader, but a spiritual Savior. Her Son would not come merely to save one race of mankind living in one historical circumstance, but He would live and die for all men everywhere and at all times. He would come to end our weeping and pain, to conquer death on our behalf.

The salvation that Christ our Lord offers us ends *the torrents of our weeping*, because God has promised us a place where no tears can be found, only forgiveness, acceptance, and love. Jesus said, "Blessed are those who mourn, for they shall be comforted" (Matthew 5:4). Blessed? Are we indeed blessed when we mourn? This present verse from the

Paraklesis tells us we are—but how? The Theotokos has given birth to our salvation, One who takes away *all tears from every face*. We are blessed when we mourn because the Theotokos gave birth to the One who came specifically for us, for those of us who carry wounds of mourning. When you mourn, you come to the attention of God. He offers you comfort. If you mourn for your sins, He offers forgiveness. If you mourn because of a loss, He offers hope. If you mourn for the fallen world, you join Him in mourning and in your mourning you become like God, a fellow laborer with Him.

It's mourning with a purpose, because it brings you to the One who ends all mourning, *for He is Christ indeed*.

> *Do thou, O Virgin Maiden, fill my heart with gladness, for thou art she who received all the fullness of joy and made to vanish away all sorrow of sinfulness.*

The words *sorrow of sinfulness* describe two different results of sin. First, our sorrow comes from the invariable consequences of sin: suffering and death. Sin produces nothing else, and always produces one or both of these. Each time we sin, we set into motion a series of events that spreads these consequences like a wildfire or a bad smell. Sin is like jumping off a building. Imagine someone going to the top of a building in order to end his own life. He goes to the edge and jumps. Part of the way down, he begins to regret his decision and repents, crying out to God for mercy. He receives mercy—but does God suddenly reverse the law of gravity? Does the man, at the moment mercy touches his soul, begin to float gently through the air? No, of course not. In spite of the fact that we change our minds and repent after we sin, we still suffer the consequences. This is one part of the sorrow of sinfulness.

But we bear a second consequence of sin along with suffering and death: a broken relationship with God. This is much worse than the primary consequences of sin, although the remorseful man plummeting toward the sidewalk might disagree. He feels like he would give everything to reverse the decision he made—but in a way, he has reversed it. When he cries out to God for mercy, this man reverses his previous opinions and decisions. He declares that life is worth living, that the future has hope, that life is more than just a biological function, and so on. He declares these new beliefs in the few seconds before he goes to stand before the judgment seat of Christ, and his soul is saved. The sorrow of his sinful decision vanishes in a wave of forgiveness and peace.

This present verse from the Paraklesis refers to the second kind of sorrow of sinfulness, our lost relationship with our Creator. By saying that the Theotokos received the *fullness of joy*, we declare that she received the One who forgives us of our sin, who can restore our relationship with the Father. She received the fullness of joy, and passed Him on to us. As a result of this gift to the world, we have a remedy for our sorrow, and our hearts are filled with gladness.

A haven and protection and a wall unshaken and a rejoicing and shelter and place of retreat dost thou become, O thou Virgin, for those who flee to thee.

This verse describes the Theotokos as a place where we might go when we're running away from the enemy and we have to hide. She is a *haven*, a *protection*, a sturdy *wall*, a *shelter*, a *place of retreat*.

But this verse also describes her as a *rejoicing*. We do not simply run to the Mother of God because we have nowhere else to turn; we run to her because she is a source of joy and celebration. When we flee from the snares of the devil, we flee out of strength, not weakness. We flee from evil out of our sense of hope, not despair. When we say that the Theotokos is a retreat for us, we're not saying that we have to run because we're in danger of succumbing to the power of the enemy. We seek the Theotokos as a retreat in a spirit of wisdom and confidence.

I can remember many times in my own life when I've had to leave situations behind—walk out of someone's house, stop talking to a particular person or socializing with a group of people, or even leave a job. These were situations that were detrimental to my spiritual life. In most cases, people read my motives as a sign of weakness. "Good riddance," they might say, "he was a drag anyway." I still feel that in some circumstances, I didn't find walking away as hard as knowing what people were saying after I left. Can I ever explain myself in such circumstances? No. If the people I left behind could understand the explanation, I probably wouldn't have had to cut off relationship with them for the sake of my soul.

I have to remind myself when I revive these memories that I walked away out of a reserve of strength, not weakness. If I'm walking through a forest and a hungry bear starts to chase me, do I think of myself as weak when I discover I can outrun him? Hardly. There are times when the best strength is a quick pair of legs.

What should you run away from? A television or radio program, a relationship or habit, an attitude or way of spending time? The Theotokos is the place for you to run to, your place of retreat. Go there, and rejoice in her light.

> *Illumine with the radiance of thy light, O Virgin, all those who piously call thee the Mother of God, and do thou banish away all darkness of ignorance.*

We refer to Mary, the Mother of our Lord Jesus Christ, as the "Mother of God." As we have noted before, any Bible-believing Christian would have no objection to this title. And this is an important aspect of everything we've said about the Theotokos in these reflections: we do not stretch the truth of Mary's value for Christians, we do not add events to her life or make up legends about her and claim that they are true. All that the Church believes about Mary, and all that we sing about her when we sing the Paraklesis, is true and authentic.

This is why I prefer to call the feast the Orthodox Church celebrates on August 15 the "Dormition" rather than the "Assumption." The beliefs concerning the bodily translation of the Theotokos (the meaning of the word "assumption") developed in the Church from the fourth to sixth centuries, during the era when the world struggled with questions around the person and nature of Christ. Stories began to circulate describing miraculous events at the funeral of the Theotokos: the sudden assembling of the Apostles from all the ends of the earth, the crippling of an enemy of the Church who tried to destroy the solemnity of the commemoration, and the eventual discovery that the body of Mary had resurrected and would not stay in the grave. What do we know of these beliefs? We know that many pious and holy people have held them throughout the Christian era. But what can we say about the Theotokos with absolute certainty? What do we know from our own experience? We know that she was the Mother of our Lord and God Incarnate, Jesus Christ, and that she died on the day we call August 15. Thus we call this day the "Dormition," expressing simply that it is the commemoration of her falling asleep. "Assumption" describes great and awesome mysteries to which no one of us can claim to be a witness. It names one part of the events around the death of the Theotokos, and the most mysterious part at that. How can we explain the discovery that her body was not in the grave after her burial, that which would have been the most valuable relic in the history of the Church?

We who come from a culture that holds the virtue of observation and exactitude very highly take great comfort and spiritual pleasure in knowing that nothing we believe about Mary the Mother of Jesus may be deemed an "old wives' tale" or a superstition. The *darkness of ignorance* we ask her to *banish* away speaks of the unwillingness of some Christians to believe this, and to honor her.

> *Brought low am I, O Virgin, in a place of sickness and in a dwelling of anguish; grant healing to me, transforming all of my illness into full healthfulness.*

Whenever I sing this verse, it makes me think that the Paraklesis sure ends on a dour note. If I had written it, I might have gone for one last great flourish of theology about the Theotokos in the last verse. Or a movie ending as we finish this beautiful prayer and exit the church in order to go back to normal life.

But the Paraklesis does not end that way. It ends with *sickness, anguish*, and *illness*. Even when we sing this great canon during the Virgin's Lent as a kind of spiritual discipline, the words themselves remind us that the reason people sing the Paraklesis is that they need help. People don't sing this, normally, just to sing it. They sing it because they have no other answer to their problems.

And this reminds us: we have no other answer either, none of us. You may not feel sick right now, and you may have no threat to your very life that you know about. But you and I both are brought low by the sickness of sin, and by the anguish caused by our own selfishness and greed. Other verses of the Paraklesis have warned us about this need, but the best reminder for us is to finish the hymn with these words: *Brought low am I, O Virgin . . . Grant healing to me.*

Scripture Reading:

Luke 8:16–21

"No one, when he has lit a lamp, covers it with a vessel or puts it under a bed, but sets it on a lampstand, that those who enter may see the light. For nothing is secret that will not be revealed, nor anything hidden that will not be known and come to light. Therefore take heed how you hear. For whoever has, to him more will be given; and whoever does not have, even what he seems to have will be taken from him."

Then His mother and brothers came to Him, and could not approach Him because of the crowd. And it was told Him by some, who said, "Your mother and Your brothers are standing outside, desiring to see You."

But He answered and said to them, "My mother and My brothers are these who hear the word of God and do it."

What a great gift we have been given in honoring the Mother of God! How can we hide it from the world?

Chapter Twelve

The Fast Doesn't Start on the First Day of the Fast

At the beginning of every Lenten season (always at Lent, but it happens before other fasts as well), I have people tell me that they've decided to "give up" something as a way of keeping the fast. Sometimes they say that they're too fat and intend to give up candy, or overeating. Perhaps they drink too much coffee and decide to give that up, or smoking, or gambling, or watching television. One woman said to me, "I'm going to give up criticizing myself about the little things and learn to accept myself for who I am." Wow! I didn't even know where to start with a response to that one!

Normally, I try to communicate to the people who tell me these kinds of things that the strictures of the fast have already been decided by the Church: abstain from meat, dairy products, fish, alcohol, and oil. No one has to think about what to give up. It's already been decided. They should, I suggest, spend their energy trying to keep the fast and give up trying to reinvent it. Why do we love to make the proven traditions of the Church easier? When generations of Christians before us have found these guidelines to be perfect, why do we want to change them? Are we more holy than they, or more intelligent?

But at the same time, I'm realistic about the number of people who fast in the Church. I know that many people in the Church do not keep the fast. Some only fast on particular days, some don't avoid all the foods that the Church tells us to avoid, and some convince themselves that they "cannot" fast at all. Sometimes these people tell me that their doctor has said that they cannot keep the fast, but when I respond to this excuse by asking them to have their doctor drop me a short note saying he advises them against fasting, I understand that no note will come my way. It's frustrating for me to talk to people about fasting, because many have set their attitudes so firmly that they cannot listen to any advice or teaching on the subject.

I'm not going to fool myself into thinking that everyone keeps the fast. So what can I do? Play mind games and pretend that everyone is fasting, that they avoid talking to me during the fast because they're busy praying? Or do I try to remain realistic, and try to bring people gradually toward obedience to the Church's teachings on this issue? It's harder to be realistic. I have to know where each person stands, and what they're capable of. So, when I know the person I'm speaking to cannot or will not fast, I suggest the very thing that I opened this chapter with: "At least," I say, "give up something." This is not the true fast, I know. But if I can see that a man has set himself against fasting, at least I want him to experience the essence of fasting. I want him to know the goal, the reason for, and the true benefit of fasting. And what is the essence of fasting? I'll use myself as an example.

When I come to the first day of a fast, I'll be honest with you, I'm excited and happy that the day has arrived. I love the first day of a fast—doesn't everyone? Isn't the first day the day of hope, the day of victory, the day of conquering the passions with little effort? I wake up in the morning and make some toast with peanut butter. Or perhaps cook oatmeal and eat it dry. Or perhaps I have some fruit and nuts. Or nothing at all, a cup of coffee or two and I'm ready to start my day. At lunch, I might have some soup, carefully prepared so that it conforms to the fast, or a peanut butter and jelly sandwich. And then dinner—I am married to the best fasting-cook in all of the Christian world, and sometimes the meals we have in our home are so wonderful that it's almost like we're not fasting at all.

Then, as I say my prayers before bed, I mentally pat myself on the back—day one, completed. Perfect.

Then day two—no problem. Day three—going strong. Day four— excellent. Day five—I think it's actually getting easier! Day six—I'm nailing this! Satan—talk to the hand! I'm not even tempted! Day seven— one week down and I'm still in a sprint!

But then, sometime in the second week, I may be driving from here to there in my work as a pastor, and I'm hungry. "I'll just hurry into a drive-through and eat a burger on my way," I decide. I pull into a fast-food place, and take my place in line. I'm thinking of something, distracted. Perhaps I hear the little voice in my head and perhaps I don't. But it's there, and it gets louder and louder until I can't ignore it: "You're fasting. You can't get anything here except a Coke." What do I do?

That's when the fasting starts. Fasting doesn't start on the first day of the fast. I don't encounter the essence of fasting simply by avoiding food or certain kinds of food. I can do that, even for as much as a week, and the only accomplishment is that I feel really proud of myself. Is that what the Church wants of me, that I would feel proud of myself? Is that why I fast, is that my Lenten discipline? Not a chance. I fast in order to encounter that moment when I no longer want to fast. When it's no longer a pleasure, a fun challenge, a game. At that moment, I come face to face with my own sinfulness, my slavery to my appetites, my spiritual immaturity, my total reliance on the grace of God. It's a hard lesson, and it makes me angry. Perhaps I start arguing with myself: "Who cares if you eat some meat? Who will know? Besides, today is a busy and difficult day, and you need your strength. I fasted all of last week, isn't that enough?" And so on.

This is the essence of fasting, that I might encounter myself. Of course, I pull my car out of line and go off down the street toward my appointment, feeling the emptiness in my stomach and the turmoil in my soul. At least I drove away. But temptation will happen again, perhaps even later that day. And the next, and the next as well. I do not encounter the essence of fasting in the short term, but over time, more than a week. Someone asked me one time why the Orthodox have four long fasts per year. Why not, she said, simply have total fast every now and then? The answer is easy. The short total fast is an ego-booster, a retreat from the world, often a team effort, a nurturer of pride. But the long fast is different. At some point, you'll find yourself frustrated and annoyed by the fast, and that's when it becomes a revealer of the self, an uncoverer of sinfulness, a temptation toward self-rule, and a true spiritual discipline.

I call this moment "the bottom," and the discipline of fasting I call "raising the bottom." I get this characterization from the parable of the Prodigal Son, which is read in the church just before the Lenten fast starts. In this parable, a son takes his inheritance from his father while his father is still alive, then moves away, only to squander the entire sum on loose living. When he is totally destitute, the son decides to go back to the father and ask for forgiveness. He does so, and the father welcomes him with open arms. It's a parable of repentance that illustrates how God waits for each of us to come to our senses so that we repent and return to Him. And when does the son repent? He repents when he hits "the bottom." He repents when he sees that he has acted like a fool, has squandered a great inheritance, has forsaken the good life. He can go no further down—he's sitting in a field with a bunch of pigs wishing they would politely offer him some of their food.

We also must come to the bottom before we repent. But do we really need to lose everything we have every time we need to return to the Father? Anyone could recognize faithful Christians if that were the case—they would be the ones whose lives are a constant tragedy! Rather than this, God gives us the fast, so that we can come to the place of knowing our sinfulness, foolishness, wastefulness, and want of life without losing everything we own. But we need to experience this. We cannot simply sit in church and say, "I'm bad, I'm a worm, I need God, I'm sinful," and expect our consequent return to the Father to be as heartfelt or authentic as the Prodigal Son's. Not in the least. We may have spoken the words of someone who has reached the bottom, but we haven't really reached the bottom ourselves. When we say words of repentance without experiencing them, our minds are concentrated on other things: "What teams are playing today? Who is that new family over there? What was the funny sound I heard in my car this morning? Church is boring," and so on. Or, when we're really serious about repentance, we might try to summon the feelings that someone at the bottom might have, and perhaps even work in a few tears to match. But actors can make themselves cry, and all we're doing is acting when we try to repent without experiencing the bottom for ourselves.

Fasting "raises the bottom." It gives us the opportunity to say, with the Prodigal Son, "I now see that I need to return to the Father," without making us sit in a field with a bunch of pigs. Without taking our families from us, or making us destitute. Fasting makes us destitute in soul, angry and frustrated with our appetites, crushed by the passions, and makes our return to the Father that much more real.

This is why I sometimes encourage parishioners to "give up something" for Lent. If someone says they'll give up the TV, I know that eventually that person will wander into the room in his house where the TV is and think about turning it on. Perhaps he'll pick up the remote, and aim it toward the TV. And what then? Of course, if that person has fasted according to the rules of the Church, he probably has the spiritual strength to stick to the additional disciplines he has laid upon himself. And if he hasn't, he probably doesn't. The struggle might seem insignificant to you as you're reading this. But when you're in front of the temptation, remote in hand, all alone, thumb over the power button, you may very well find yourself overwhelmed by your sinfulness and slavery to your appetites. It's a humbling experience, the bottom.

Prayer must accompany fasting. These two experiences are like a pair of shoes, identical but different. Can you think yourself prepared to start your day when you have only one shoe on? One glove? If your car's gas tank is full, but it has no oil? Fasting without prayer is the fulfilling of a rule that will not bring you any closer to the Lord. It's like lifting your hands without prayer, opening the Bible without reading, going to church only to drink coffee and eat donuts in the hall while the liturgy is celebrated in the church. The start is good, but the conclusion is not reached. Fasting is good, but without prayer it has little spiritual benefit. "Food will not commend us to God," St. Paul tells us, and neither will the absence of certain kinds of food.

Fasting is a negative action. It's the only spiritual exercise that consists of not doing something. And so the devil whispers to you, "If you eat peanut butter and jelly for lunch rather than bologna, you'll become a good person." Yes. As with most lies, this is partly true. Fasting is a good thing. But will you encounter its essence without prayer? Without some vehicle for self-reflection? The essence of fasting only gains its full spiritual impact through the spiritual discipline of prayer.

And along with fasting and prayer, the fulfillment of self-reflection happens in the sacrament of repentance. The Prodigal Son used his realization of his sinfulness to prepare his speech of repentance, and then he made his way to the Father. What would have happened if he had stopped at fasting and self-reflection, as he sat in the muddy field like one more unit of livestock? Nothing at all. Perhaps his bones would still sit there today, under layers and years of dirt and compost. But no! He stood and walked toward the Father, with his plan for repentance in his mouth. And when the Father came to embrace him, he did not return the embrace until he had expressed the depths of his sin. The return needed to be spoken forth before the forgiveness could be complete.

This is also the message of St. John the Baptist. What one-word piece of advice did he leave as his legacy, his offering, his icon? "Repent!" What one-word sermon did he give to Christians of all generations? "Repent!" The people who crossed the Jordan in first-century Palestine made a spiritual journey in order to hear St. John say one word to them. They traveled in groups, enjoying the chance to step out of their ordinary lives and do something special to feed their souls. The wilderness was dry and hot, and the disciples of the Forerunner sometimes had to help people who suffered exhaustion, or encourage those in the crowds to help one another. They came to weep, to hear the saint say things that would prick their consciences and make them sensitive to sin.

"Repent!" he said, and this means you. In the sacrament of confession, you sharpen your sensitivity to sin. Sometimes people say to their priest that they don't believe they need to go to confession in order to be forgiven. They're right! They need instead to go to confession in order to speak their sins, to feel the weight of sin, its ridiculous nature, its monotony, its determination to draw us away from our saving God. You go to confession in order to hear with your own ears some advice, to hear a human being pray that God would forgive you. Of course, God will forgive you your sins when you cry them to Him alone in your bedroom. But your ability to detect the pernicious grip of sin in your life, its wiles and techniques, its strategy for defeating your every attempt to become a righteous person is sharpened by the advice of the one who hears your confession—either the priest of God who knows and loves you, and longs even to give his life that you might experience God's forgiving grace, or the unresponsive pillow under your head, which sometimes offers a certain kind of rest, but speaks forth no hope at all.

Scripture Reading:
Mark 9:17–29

Then one of the crowd answered and said, "Teacher, I brought You my son, who has a mute spirit. And whenever it seizes him, it throws him down; he foams at the mouth, gnashes his teeth, and becomes rigid. So I spoke to Your disciples, that they should cast it out, but they could not."

He answered him and said, "O faithless generation, how long shall I be with you? How long shall I bear with you? Bring him to Me."

Then they brought him to Him. And when he saw Him, immediately the spirit convulsed him, and he fell on the ground and wallowed, foaming at the mouth. So He asked his father, "How long has this been happening to him?" And he said, "From childhood. And often he has thrown him both into the fire and into the water to destroy him. But if You can do anything, have compassion on us and help us."

Jesus said to him, "If you can believe, all things are possible to him who believes."

Immediately the father of the child cried out and said with tears, "Lord, I believe; help my unbelief!"

When Jesus saw that the people came running together, He rebuked the unclean spirit, saying to it, "Deaf and dumb spirit, I command you, come out of him and enter him no more!"

Then the spirit cried out, convulsed him greatly, and came out of him. And he became as one dead, so that many said, "He is dead."

But Jesus took him by the hand and lifted him up, and he arose. And when He had come into the house, His disciples asked Him privately, "Why could we not cast it out?"

So He said to them, "This kind can come out by nothing but prayer and fasting."

After two little speeches (speeches which only seemed to annoy the Lord), this man finally "hit the bottom," and shouted in desperation, "Lord, I believe; help my unbelief!" This admission of his own powerlessness opened the way for him to receive the blessing of his son's healing from the Lord.

Later on, the disciples asked how the healing had been accomplished. On one level, Jesus tells them that they will gain spiritual insight and ability from prayer and fasting. But on another level, Jesus alerts them and us to the fact that prayer and fasting can reduce us to the desperation that the father of the sick boy needed in order to accept healing.

We do not, therefore, embrace a season of prayer and fasting in order to gain super-spiritual powers, but in order to learn to cry out sincerely: "Lord I believe; help my unbelief!"

Chapter Thirteen

The Transfiguration of Our Lord

I vividly remember the frustration I felt as I sat with a family whose house I had just blessed. The mother wanted me to answer a question her children had asked about Jesus, and (because it was early January) I began by saying to the boys, "We just celebrated the Nativity, the celebration of the birth of Jesus, who is God Incarnate . . ."

The mother quickly interjected, "Not God. The Son of God."

"Yes," I said, taking my attention from the children to respond to her interruption, "we also call Jesus the Son of God, but all the Persons of the Trinity are God, they are all one—one God." She looked back at me, registering nothing, so I turned to her sons. "As I was saying, Jesus is God . . ."

Again, the mom broke in. "Not God. The Son of God."

I looked over at her again. "We are talking about the same thing. God is God, whether it's the eternal Father or the coeternal Son. They are one God." I waited for a moment to see if she would argue with what I had just said, then again turned to the children. I simply said the words, "Jesus is God," to see if she would interrupt.

She did, quickly saying, "Not God. Jesus is the Son of God." And again, that's all she said.

What could I do? Obviously, someone had taught this woman, perhaps when she was no older than her own boys sitting in front of me that day, that Jesus was and is not God. She expressed her belief that the Son of God differs somehow from God the Father in terms of divinity, to the extent that she regarded the statement "Jesus is God" as wrong.

Her error, of course, is the ancient Arian heresy, in which Jesus is declared less than God, part of God's creation and not the Creator Himself. It makes some logical sense, in a way, that some people think this.

It offends our rational minds to think that God could become a man, at least in the way Christians claim Jesus did. How could the omnipresent God, who fills and sustains all things, live in a human body?

Indeed, heretics ancient and modern are not the only ones who have trouble understanding the Incarnation. Our Lord knew that His own disciples would forget His divinity when they found themselves under the pressure of His arrest, trial, and crucifixion. Because He knew this, He gave them the Transfiguration. In fact, I handled the frustrating interruptions of the mother in my story by bringing her to the Scriptures that describe the Transfiguration. She listened quietly to what I said, nodding her head, and then let me answer her children's questions (which had nothing to do with the divinity of Christ) with no interruptions. I often wonder if she gave them a little lecture of her own after I left: "The priest doesn't know what he's talking about. Jesus is the Son of God, not God."

What is so hard to believe about the Incarnation? Many things. It's hard to believe that the disciples, ordinary men, heard the voice of God and looked directly into His eyes. It's hard to imagine how God could walk on the ground in Galilee and at the same time be present everywhere and fill all things. It's hard to imagine that God did not simply occupy a body that He used and then disposed of when He didn't need it any longer, but that He suffered in the flesh as a central part of His mission of salvation.

This same God spoke to Moses, and Moses longed to see His face. In the Old Testament Book of Exodus, we have an account of Moses trying to look upon the God whom he served:

And he said, "Please, show me Your glory."

Then He said, "I will make all My goodness pass before you, and I will proclaim the name of the LORD before you. I will be gracious to whom I will be gracious, and I will have compassion on whom I will have compassion."

But He said, "You cannot see My face; for no man shall see Me, and live." And the LORD said, "Here is a place by Me, and you shall stand on the rock. So it shall be, while My glory passes by, that I will put you in the cleft of the rock, and will cover you with My hand while I pass by. Then I will take away My hand, and you shall see My back; but My face shall not be seen." (Exodus 33:18–23)

Even Moses could not look at the face of God, but some first-century Roman soldiers did indeed look at it, slap it, spit on it, and drove nail-sized thorns into the divine head. How could this be?

In order for our Lord to impart the full weight of this truth to the disciples, He took three of them up to Mount Tabor where they could see His glory, teaching them that His arrest and crucifixion would not take God by surprise the way it would take them by surprise, but that it would be part of His divine plan for the world:

Thou wast transfigured on the mount,
and Thy Disciples, insofar as they were able,
beheld Thy glory, O Christ our God;
so that, when they should see Thee crucified,
they would remember that Thy suffering was voluntary,
and could declare to all the world
that Thou art truly the effulgent splendor of the Father.
(Kontakion of the Transfiguration)

They would see on Mount Tabor the normally unseen glory of God Incarnate, the very thing that Moses asked to see.

When we celebrate this feast, we commemorate not only this particular historical event, but also the possibility that the event expresses for us. It's like celebrating a birthday, in a way. We commemorate birthdays on the day that a person was born, and that's an expression of an historical fact. But we also celebrate the person, the friend or family member, showing that person our love with some kind of recognition befitting that person's age. That's the present reality. So it is when we celebrate feasts in the Church. We sing hymns and read the scriptures related to the historical event. But we also look to the meaning of the historical event for our own souls. What does it mean to us that three men were able to see the glory of God on that mountain so long ago?

To answer this question, look again at the words of the Kontakion above. The disciples beheld the glory of God "insofar as they were able."

We cannot see the glory of God without ability. And how did the disciples gain that ability? They lived constantly with Jesus, listening to Him, talking with Him, allowing Him to reveal their faults, begging His forgiveness, serving Him. So it is with us. We do not see the glory of God based on a snap decision. Only three of the disciples had the ability to see the glory of God, as much as their ability allowed. What could lead us to believe that we spend more time with Jesus than St. Matthew, or St. Thomas, or any of the other disciples the Lord left at the bottom of Mount Tabor?

So the first meaning of the Transfiguration has to do with the closeness of God, and the call that He makes for us to persevere in the faith, always climbing higher, continually calling His presence to mind, praying always and giving thanks to Him for all things. When we do, God rewards us with His presence and glory. He stands close to us, next to us, filling us and surrounding us. We are in Him, and He in us, like a man underwater who is filled with water, indeed, made almost entirely of water. He makes Himself available to us so that we may drown in Him.

The second meaning of the Transfiguration has to do with the benefit of following hard after God, which is to behold His glory. The three disciples had just climbed a mountain before the vision of glory, but when the glory of God appeared to them, did their legs suddenly gain new strength and their feet stop hurting? Did they begin to float so that they didn't have to stand any more? Did they suddenly become geniuses—healthy, happy geniuses? No, certainly not. In fact, the Gospels record an informative exchange between our Lord and St. Peter right after the vision of glory, when St. Peter shows that he clearly did not understand the meaning of the event. So what benefit did he gain? What good things came to St. Peter for the fact that he had just seen the very glory of God Himself?

The benefit and the reward is the glory itself. The glory is the truth of the universe. The glory is the reality of God, the fellowship of the Trinity. In beholding the glory of God, we behold all that makes us whole, just as the three disciples with the Lord experienced the closest fellowship with God that anyone on earth can have. Later on, St. Peter demonstrated that he still didn't understand what good things the Lord had for him:

> Then Peter answered and said to Him, "See, we have left all
> and followed You. Therefore what shall we have?" So Jesus said
> to them, "Assuredly I say to you, that in the regeneration, when
> the Son of Man sits on the throne of His glory, you who
> have followed Me will also sit on twelve thrones . . ." (Matthew
> 19:27–28)

The good thing God has for us is God Himself. The good things we
wait for will be revealed to us not in this world, but in the world to come.

For a third meaning of this feast, we look to the figures surrounding
our Lord, Moses and Elijah. They bow to Christ, and bring the entire
history of God's dealing with man into the feast. Since the beginning of
time, God planned to bring Jesus Christ to the world for the salvation
of His creation. As part of this plan, God led men toward His Incarnation through the law, the sacrificial system, the prophets. He showed us
His love in these two Old Testament righteous ones and the grace of
God they symbolize. He showed us through them how His relationship
with men would work. And when He had prepared the world, Christ
came—not as a new teaching, not as a renewed attempt on the part of
God to reach out to the fallen world, but as the culmination of His
Divine Plan.

How important it is for us to see Moses and Elijah standing to the
right and left of our Lord in the Transfiguration! We see in their presence with Him that each moment of time and history has a meaning
and a plan. God's plan for the world and for mankind started long
before the Incarnation, and continues until today, until right now. You
are part of that plan. When you look around you, it may sometimes
seem as if God has withdrawn from the world, that He has finished His
active work and has given the world over to its own devices. But this is
not the case. We know that the Scriptures themselves speak of more to
come. Look at the Old Testament figures worshipping our Lord, and
ask: How many of the people who lived when they lived wondered if
God had forgotten the world? Many did, most did. So many did that
when our Lord came to this world, very few believed that God did
anything anymore. But now we know that God continues to work His
plan for the world, and we await the coming manifestations of His glory
patiently.

Scripture Reading:
2 Peter 1:10–19

Therefore, brethren, be even more diligent to make your call and election sure, for if you do these things you will never stumble; for so an entrance will be supplied to you abundantly into the everlasting kingdom of our Lord and Savior Jesus Christ.

For this reason I will not be negligent to remind you always of these things, though you know and are established in the present truth. Yes, I think it is right, as long as I am in this tent, to stir you up by reminding you, knowing that shortly I must put off my tent, just as our Lord Jesus Christ showed me. Moreover I will be careful to ensure that you always have a reminder of these things after my decease.

For we did not follow cunningly devised fables when we made known to you the power and coming of our Lord Jesus Christ, but were eyewitnesses of His majesty. For He received from God the Father honor and glory when such a voice came to Him from the Excellent Glory: "This is My beloved Son, in whom I am well pleased." And we heard this voice which came from heaven when we were with Him on the holy mountain.

And so we have the prophetic word confirmed, which you do well to heed as a light that shines in a dark place, until the day dawns and the morning star rises in your hearts.

When St. Peter wants to tell his readers about the time when he witnessed the majesty of Christ, he reminds them of the Transfiguration (vv. 17–18). And so by seeking nothing other than the glory of God, we also learn to witness His majesty.

Chapter Fourteen

The Dormition of the Theotokos

I want to introduce you (or reintroduce you, should you have been blessed by its words already) to a wonderful poem by Rainer Maria Rilke. Actually, not the whole poem, but one section of a poem entitled "Of the Death of Mary," one work in a collection entitled *The Life of the Virgin Mary*. Rilke writes from a kind of German Romanticism to which I don't always relate, but I have always kept his poetry close at hand (especially at the Feast of the Dormition) because Rilke expresses such a beautiful love for the Theotokos. I find my own love for our Lord's Mother blessed and enhanced by his brilliant and mysterious images.

> Who has considered that until her coming
> the manifold heaven was incomplete?
> The resurrected one had taken his place,
> but next him, throughout four and twenty years,
> the seat was empty. And already they began
> to grow accustomed to the clean gap that was
> as if healed over, for with his beautiful
> overspreading shine the Son filled it.
>
> So even she, entering the heavens, went
> not towards him, much as she longed to. There was
> no room there, only He was there, resplendent
> with a radiance that hurt her.
> Yet as she now, that moving figure,
> joined the newly blessed and took her place,
> inconspicuous, light to light,

there broke out of her being a withheld store
of such glory, that the angel lightened up
by her cried out dazzled: Who is she?
Amazement reigned. Then they all saw how
above God the Father withheld our Lord
so that, with mild twilight playing round it,
the empty place showed like a bit of sorrow,
a trace of loneliness, like something
he was still enduring, a residue
of earthly time, a dried-up canker—.
They looked towards her: she was watching anxiously,
leaning far out, as though she felt: I am
his longest pain—: and suddenly plunged forward.
But the angels took her to themselves
and supported her and sang beatifically
and carried her the last stretch aloft.[2]

The subtitle of the poem "Of the Death of Mary" is "Three Pieces," and this is the second of the three that I read every year just before the Feast of the Dormition. Rilke begins by describing the scene in heaven between the Ascension and the death of Mary, in which Christ enthroned sits next to a second throne that was made for, and waits for, His Mother. Ever since the Ascension, long enough that the citizens of heaven had already "grown accustomed to the clean gap," it sat empty. The light of Christ overshadowed everything to the degree that it almost seemed as if it should always remain that way.

Rilke puts in words a characteristic of the Dormition that we can see in the Orthodox icons depicting this feast. Look at the icon on page 113. Christ stands as the central figure. He holds a small Mary, an icon of her soul, in striking contrast to the ordinary depictions of the Theotokos in which she holds the infant Christ in her arms. But we see in this icon more than just the fact that our Lord welcomed His Mother's soul to heaven. We also see the reunion of Mother and Son. Did He appear to her while she still walked the earth, as He did to St. Paul when

---

2 Norton, M. D. Herter, translator, *Translations from the Poetry of Rainer Maria Rilke* (New York: W. W. Norton and Company, 1938, reissued 1993).

the great apostle was learning about the new Christian faith? Or did he wait those "four and twenty years," the throne next to Him empty, until her body finished its earthly work and ascended as He Himself had done? While we live in this flesh, we will never know. But Rilke invites us at least to meditate on the mystery of this reunion: "Who has considered that until her coming the manifold heaven was incomplete?" he asks. When you read the poem through and consider its meaning, you become one who can answer, "I have."

Then, as the Theotokos enters heaven, she does not immediately approach her Son. Rather, she makes her way to a humble place, quietly, inconspicuously, as if to join the ranks of the blessed simply as any other human might. An angel near her, however, cannot help but see the brilliance of her glory, and wonders who she is.

Again, a central aspect of the Theotokos is expressed—her humility. In our scripture reading for today, notice how much the Incarnation is linked to the question of the humility of our Lord: "being found in appearance as a man, He humbled himself" (Philippians 2:8). All humans have needs and functions that keep us humble. When I look at the icon of the Dormition, in which Christ welcomes His Mother to heaven holding her as He might a child, I'm reminded of the last months of my own father's life. He lived with my family for his last seven months before he died of Alzheimer's Disease. Many things about our bodies humble us, but perhaps none as much as growing old, when our children must become our parents, complete with all the messy accouterments of infancy. Our bodies humble us—who can imagine that God took one for himself? And yet He did, a gift from His Mother to Him and to us. Mary grasped the mystery even before the angels sang the Nativity praises that terrified the shepherds. She understood that the essence of the Incarnation was humility, and she took this virtue for herself in order to teach it to the infant, the toddler, the boy, and the young man, our Lord Jesus Christ. Where else would He have learned it?

And where can we learn it? Where can we learn humility? Once I had a man working for me who could not stand the perceived arrogance of his coworkers. They had worked at the job longer—he was only with us for the summer—and so they had some authority over him. As we talked, I could tell that this young man just didn't like to be told what to do. I asked him about his other jobs. Did he find himself working in the past with people who made him want to quit? He said yes. I told him that I thought God kept putting annoying people in his path so that he would learn humility. Would he rise to God's challenge, and overcome his own pride?

Each of us encounters obstacles that slow us down and work to keep us humble. We can't necessarily see it happening in other people's lives, because we all like to keep these kinds of things hidden, but it happens to everyone. How do we handle these obstacles, from little things like the weather to big disasters, illnesses, or downright evil people in our lives? We have the Theotokos as our model, our inspiration, our hope, aid, and pilot. When we ignore her example, we mutter, fight, sue, gossip, and stew, and once we've started it's hard to stop. The young man who worked for me during that summer long ago went on to start his own business because he couldn't hear my advice, and his pride kept him from working with, or under, anyone. Perhaps God has stopped trying to reach him, because at least financially his arrogance has served him well.

Back to Rilke's poem. Our Lord longs to go to His Mother as soon as she's identified, when in heaven "amazement reigned." But He's held back by the Father. For a moment the empty throne shines, and the longing between the separated members of the family—the Father, the Mother, the Son—burns. Then she starts toward Him, walking at first. She is soon swept up and carried by angels.

Again, Rilke expressed in these few words a central aspect of the Christian life, that it is a faith built on relationship—not on law, ritual, or logic. God the Father has entered into a close relationship with a human being, the Theotokos, in order to effect our salvation from sin. He is the Father and she is the Mother of a Son, the coeternal Second Person of the one Triune God. Mary is not a part of the Trinity, but as the Mother of Jesus, Son of the Eternal Father, she is the one of all mankind closest to the inner workings of God.

And so with us. We do not achieve salvation by knowing certain things or owning certain talismans, but by having a relationship with a Person, Jesus Christ the Savior. Thanks to God that He came to this earth to reach sinful people like you and me, and thanks to the one who brought Him to us, Mary His Mother, the Theotokos and God-bearer.

Scripture Reading:
Philippians 2:5–11

Let this mind be in you which was also in Christ Jesus, who, being in the form of God, did not consider it robbery to be equal with God, but made Himself of no reputation, taking the form of a bondservant, and coming in the likeness of men. And being found in appearance as a man, He humbled Himself and became obedient to the point of death, even the death of the cross. Therefore God also has highly exalted Him and given Him the name which is above every name, that at the name of Jesus every knee should bow, of those in heaven, and of those on earth, and of those under the earth, and that every tongue should confess that Jesus Christ is Lord, to the glory of God the Father.

As we consider the mystery of the Mother of God, let us recall the mind of Christ, His humility and servanthood, and give glory to His Mother, who taught Him these virtues.

About the Author:

Fr. David Smith and his wife, Donna, have four children and live in Utica, New York, where he is the pastor of St. George Antiochian Orthodox Church.